# Message to the Motorist:  STOP and READ

 P9-CRG-280

Safe and responsible driving begins with you! Be a safe driver and drive defensively. Being a defensive driver means bringing knowledge, skills and the right attitude to driving safely.

This study guide will teach you about road signs, traffic laws, safe driving, responsible driving, and how to get and keep your driver's licence.

This study guide is one of many sources to give you the skills and knowledge you need for getting your G1 and G2 and becoming a fully licensed Class G driver in Ontario. It uses terms and language that are fairly easy to understand by the general public. However, it is also recommended you consult other sources for more specific information.

For official law descriptions and administrative centres, consult these sources:

- The Ontario Ministry of Transportation, www.mto.gov.on.ca

  **Note: Laws are constantly changing so obtain the most recent news from the Ministry of Transportation.**

- Highway Traffic Act, www.e-laws.gov.on.ca

- Drive Test, www.drivetest.ca

It is also highly recommended that all new drivers take an approved driver education course to gain positive driving habits and learn and perfect the skills needed for safe, defensive driving.

**Education, practice, commitment to safety and observing the rules and advice in this study guide and other sources will help you get and stay on the road safely.**

# How to Use This Study Guide

Read everything carefully. The **sample test questions** numbered 1–201 and the **G2 Exit Test section** are designed to help you get your Class G1, G2 and G licence. **Please note: This study guide is for general reference only; consult the Ministry of Transportation for more detailed information.**

**Questions 1–92** are about traffic signs such as regulatory, warning and temporary signs. You will be asked some of these questions on the written knowledge test. **Please note: The way some of these questions are asked will vary. For example, sometimes a traffic sign will be shown and other times a traffic sign will**

be described with text. So read this study guide carefully and make sure you know and understand all the information.

**Questions 93–201** are about responsible and safe driving, from what to do when you get in a car to steering out of a skid and more. These questions will help you understand what you need to know. Safe driving requires knowledge, skill gained through practice and a commitment to safety.

For each question, select the most appropriate response, without looking below at the added information section. These information boxes sometimes give the answer away. Other times they will provide you with valuable added information to help with your understanding.

*Sample question.*

145. **If you skid on a slippery road surface what shou**
    a) Steer your vehicle into the direction you want
    b) Steer your vehicle into the opposite direction
    c) Apply gas to quickly get out of the skid.
    d) Turn off the ignition.
    ⓘ Skids generally happen because a vehicle is travelling too driving accordingly.

146. **What is black ice?**
    a) When snow is mixed with mud and then free
    b) When newly paved roads are wet.
    c) When asphalt has a thin layer of ice on it.
    d) When ice is mixed with snow.
    ⓘ Black ice can form anywhere, especially on bridges which to drop more quickly on the bridge forming a thin layer of

Check your answers on the inside back cover to see how well you scored. *Could you pass?*

**Questions on the G1 Knowledge Test can include these topics:**

- ✔ Traffic signs
- ✔ Traffic lights
- ✔ Driver's licence and other documents
- ✔ Seatbelts
- ✔ Rules of the road and driving
- ✔ Using headlights
- ✔ Speed limits
- ✔ Emergency vehicles
- ✔ Entering and exiting a highway
- ✔ Passing vehicles
- ✔ Sharing the road

- ✔ Approaching an emergency vehicle, school bus, or streetcar
- ✔ Accident reporting
- ✔ The Demerit Point System
- ✔ Blood alcohol levels (BAL)
- ✔ Driving suspensions
- ✔ Vehicle safety inspections and maintenance

*Sample illustration.*

A Check mirrors and blind spots for space.
B Signal and check for space again.
C Steer into lane.
D Turn off signal.

Once you have had your G1 for 12 months, or 8 months if you have taken a Ministry-approved driver education course and passed it, you can book a G1 Exit Test in order to get a G2 level licence. You will be evaluated on what you have learned from this study guide, your driver education course and from other sources.

The **G2 Exit Test Section** explains what to bring, what you are tested on, and what the examiner looks for when you book a G2 Exit Test. Read through this section of the study guide to help prepare for your test.

# The Ontario Licensing System

To drive in Ontario you must have a valid driver's licence and it must be the right one for the vehicle you want to drive. Vehicles include cars, trucks, motorcycles, buses, etc. (see chart on page 7 for different vehicles and which type of licence is required to drive each). You must have a Class G licence before you can obtain another type of licence. The only exception is a motorcycle licence, where you

can get a Class M licence without getting a Class G licence first.

## Getting Your Class G Licence As a New Driver

Ontario has a Graduated Licensing System that requires all drivers to graduate from the first level before moving on to the next level. The Graduated Licensing process takes about 20 months to complete and allows new drivers to gain skills and experience gradually. Levels include:

### Class G1

For this level you must be 16 years old or older, pass a vision test and pass a written knowledge test of the rules of the road, including road and traffic signs. Use this study guide to help you learn about signs and rules of the road. If you pass these tests, you will increase your chances of

getting a G1 licence. Knowledge and vision tests are conducted at DriveTest Centres found at: www.drivetest.ca/EN/bookatest/Pages/LocationFinder.aspx . You do not need to make an appointment for the G1 knowledge and vision tests. Ensure you have adequate time to perform the tests. Centre hours may vary.

Once you get your Class G1 licence you must follow a number of rules at this level or risk suspension of your licence (see page 6). **Please note: Laws and therefore driving rules may change. Consult the Ministry of Transportation for up-to-date information.**

## Class G2

You must have your Class G1 licence for 12 months before trying for the next level. If, however, you take an approved driver education course and pass, you can complete your G1 in 8 months. Once you meet the full requirements of a G1 driver you can book a G1 Exit Test. The G1 Exit Test is a road driving test that tests basic driving skills. Contact Drive Test at 1-888-570-6110 to book an appointment or go online at www.irtb.rus.mto.gov.on.ca. Ensure you bring the appropriate vehicle to the road test and that it is in good working order so that it passes the examiners pre-test vehicle check.

If you pass the first road test, you will obtain your Class G2 licence. Once you obtain your G2 licence you have more driving privileges because of your driving experience. However, you must follow a new set of rules in order to not have your licence suspended (see page 6). **Please note: Laws and therefore driving rules may change. Consult the Ministry of Transportation for up-to-date information.**

## Class G

Once you have had your Class G2, or Level 2 licence for 12 months you can book a G2 Exit Test. This is a driving test that tests advanced driving knowledge and skills that you have gained through your driving experience. Before you book your Level 2 road test you must complete and sign a "Declaration of Highway Driving Experience" to show that you have adequate highway driving experience. Find out more at www.drivetest.ca. As with the G1 Exit Test, ensure you bring an appropriate vehicle for your G2 Exit Test. Ensure the vehicle is in good working order and that it would pass a pre-test vehicle check.

| G1 Rules | G2 Rules |
|---|---|
| Your blood alcohol level must be 0 while driving. | Your blood alcohol level must be 0 while driving. |
| Each passenger must have a working seatbelt on. | Each passenger must have a working seatbelt on. |
| You must not drive between midnight and 5 a.m. | If you are 19 years old or younger the following restrictions apply between midnight and 5 a.m.: You are only allowed to have 1 passenger 19 years old or younger during the first 6 months of having your G2. After 6 months have passed and until you obtain your full licence or turn 20, you are allowed to have up to 3 passengers aged 19 or under. |
| You must not drive alone. You must be accompanied by a driver with a valid Class G licence (or higher) with at least 4 years driving experience. This person must be the sole passenger in the front seat and they must have a blood alcohol level of less than .05%; 0% if they are 21 years of age or younger. | The above does not apply<br><br>• if you are accompanied by a driver with a valid Class G licence (or higher). This person must be sitting in the front seat and they must have a blood alcohol level of less than .05%; 0% if they are 21 years of age or younger.<br><br>or<br><br>• if your passengers are members of your immediate family, a guardian, or those that are related to you by blood, marriage, common law, or adoption. |
| You are not permitted to drive on the 400-series highways or high velocity expressways (QEW, Don Valley Parkway, Gardiner Expressway, E. C. Row Expressway, and the Conestoga Parkway). However, if you are with a licensed Ontario driving instructor, you can drive on any road. | |

# Licence Classification Chart

| Licence Class | | May also drive licence |
|---|---|---|
| A | Allows any tractor-trailer or a motor vehicle and towed vehicle(s) in which the towed vehicle(s) have a total weight in excess of 4,600 kg. | D, G and A with "R" condition |
| A with restricted condition "R" | Allows drivers who pass a Licence Class A road test while driving a small truck and trailer combination to drive a similar combination. The Class A restricted licence holders may not drive a motor vehicle pulling double trailers or a trailer with air-brakes. | D and G |
| B | Allows any school-purpose bus with a seating allotment for greater than 24 passengers. | C, D, E, F and G |
| C | Allows any regular bus with a seating allotment for greater than 24 passengers. | D, F and G |
| D | Allows any truck or combination as long as the towed vehicle does not exceed 4600 kg. | G |
| E | Allows any school-purpose bus with a maximum of 24 passengers. | F and G |
| F | Allows ambulances and any regular bus with a maximum of 24 passengers. | G |

| Licence Class | | May also drive licence |
|---|---|---|
| G | Allows any car, small truck or van or combination of vehicle and towed vehicle up to 11 000 kg as long as the towed vehicle is not over 4600 kg. A pick-up truck may tow a recreational vehicle exceeding 4,600 kg. | |
| G1 | Graduated licensing Level 1 holders may drive Class G vehicles with an accompanying fully licensed driver with at least 4 years' driving experience who sits in the front passenger seat. Other conditions apply. See G1 Rules on page 6. | |
| G2 | Graduated licensing Level 2 holders may drive Class G vehicles without an accompanying driver, but other conditions apply. See G2 Rules on page 6. | |
| M | Allows motorcycles, motor-assisted bicycles such as mopeds, and includes limited-speed motorcycles such as motor scooters. | M with "L" conditions |
| M1 | Motorcycle graduated licensing Level 1 includes motorcycles, motor-assisted bicycles such as mopeds, and includes limited-speed motorcycles such as motor scooters. | M with "L" conditions |
| M2 | Motorcycle graduated licensing Level 2 includes motorcycles, motor-assisted bicycles such as mopeds, and includes limited-speed motorcycles such as motor scooters. | M with "L" conditions |
| M with condition L | Permits only limited-speed motorcycles and mopeds. | |
| M2 with condition L | Permits only limited-speed motorcycles and mopeds. | |

# How to Get Your Driver's Licence

## 1. Find and Bring Personal Identification

You need to show documentation that proves your age (day, month and year), your name and your signature.

All documents must be valid and original, no photocopies. **Some examples include:**

- ✔ Passport (Canadian or foreign)
- ✔ Canadian Citizenship Card with photo
- ✔ Permanent Immigration documents
- ✔ Temporary Immigration documents

If the above documents do not prove all 3 requirements of age, name and signature, there are additional documents you may bring. These additional documents must contain proof of the missing or invalid information. For example, a Canadian or U.S. Birth Certificate is acceptable as proof of legal name and date of birth, but not valid for signature. For proof of signature some valid documents are an Ontario Student Card with signature, or an Ontario Health Card with signature.

**For a complete list of acceptable sources please log on to:** www.drivetest.ca/en/licencing/Pages/How-to-Apply.aspx .

If you still cannot come up with the required signature proof you may get a guarantor to validate your signature. From the above website download the "Declaration from a Guarantor" form. On the form is a list of guarantors you may contact to fill out and sign their portion of the form to validate your signature.

## 2. Go to a Driver Examination Centre

Bring all documents that prove your name, age and signature to your nearest DriveTest Driver Examination Centre. Find locations at: www.drivetest.ca/en/bookatest/Pages/LocationFinder.aspx .

Ensure you arrive well in advance of business close.

## 3. Pay the Required Licence Fees at the Driver Examination Centre

The fee for new drivers is $145 net, which includes a knowledge test, a G1 road test (to be booked later) and a 5-year licence. A G2 road test is $50 net. All fees are posted online at the Ontario Ministry of Transportation website. Before taking any tests at the centre you must first pay for the test by the accepted method

of payment: cash, credit card, debit card, certified cheque, money order or travellers cheque.

## 4. Answer Questions About Your Health

All driver's licence applicants are asked questions about their health. This is to ensure that you are fit to drive safely. Some people with certain medical conditions or physical challenges are not allowed to drive, for their own safety and the safety of others.

Medical and physical conditions can change at any time during your graduated and final Class G licence attainment. You must report changes about your health that may affect your ability to drive safely. You may be asked to reapply depending on your situation. Doctors and optometrists must report people who have medical and physical challenges that make driving unsafe for them.

## 5. Take the Required Test

Your knowledge of what you studied from this study guide and from other sources will be tested. You will have 40 questions to answer on the G1 knowledge test, including 20 sign and 20 driving related questions. You will be given enough time to complete the test. When you hand in your test it will be marked and you will be notified if you passed or failed right at the centre. You will also know which questions you answered incorrectly. If you failed the test you may rewrite it at any time for a small fee. If you pass, you will obtain a paper copy of your G1 licence. You will have your photo taken which will be on your official G1 licence that will be mailed to you.

## New Residents from Out of Province or Out of Country

If you have a valid driver's licence from another province, state or country, and are 16 years old or older, you can drive in

Ontario for up to 60 days before you have to apply for an Ontario Driver's Licence.

When you apply for an Ontario Driver's Licence, if you are from a country in which there is a reciprocal exchange agreement with Ontario, you will have to fulfill fewer requirements than if you were from a country not part of the agreement. Some restrictions apply, depending on which country you are from and how much driving experience you have. Find out all details from Service Ontario Driver and Vehicle Information at (416) 235-2999 or toll free in Canada at 1-800-387-3445, or look online at www.drivetest.ca.

If you are a new Ontario resident, besides meeting licence time requirements, you must also register your vehicle. New Ontario residents must register their vehicles within 30 days. Registration includes a vehicle permit and licence plates. Register at a Driver and Vehicle Licence Issuing Office. You must bring required information such as a Safety Standards Certificate, proof you have insurance and more. Find out what all the required documents are before you go.

## Visitors from Out of Province or Out of Country

If you are visiting Ontario from another province, state or country, are 16 years old or older, and have a valid driver's licence from your country, you may drive in Ontario for up to 90 days. If you are going to be in Ontario for more than 90 days and you are from out of country, you must have an International Driver's Permit from your country. If you are from out of province and will be in Ontario for more than 90 days you must apply for an Ontario Driver's Licence.

Find out all details from the phone numbers and websites listed on this page.

# Sample Test

## *Could you pass?*

Use the Practice Test Form on pages 99-100 to record your answers and then check the inside back cover to see how well you scored.

ⓘ For each question, select the most appropriate response, without looking below at the added information section. These information boxes sometimes give the answer away. Other times they will provide you with valuable added information to help with your understanding.

| | | |
|---|---|---|
| 1. | a) No stopping.<br>b) Stop if necessary and go when intersection is clear.<br>c) Come to a full stop.<br>d) Do not enter road.<br><br>ⓘ If there is no stop line, crosswalk or sidewalk, stop at the intersection edge. | |
| 2. | a) You have the right-of-way.<br>b) Give others the right-of-way.<br>c) Always stop, then yield.<br>d) Do not enter.<br><br>ⓘ Traffic in the intersection or traffic close to it goes first. Only stop if necessary, then proceed when clear. | |
| 3. | a) School zone, reduce speed to 60 km/h.<br>b) Slow down, school zone ahead, watch for children and drive with extra caution.<br>c) You are approaching a school bus loading zone.<br>d) Watch for pedestrians at crosswalk.<br><br>ⓘ School zone signs are neon yellow or blue and 5-sided. Always reduce speed and watch for children. | |
| 4. | a) This is a pedestrian crosswalk.<br>b) A railway crossing is X-shaped and filled in with red.<br>c) Deer cross this area.<br>d) A railway crossing sign indicating railway tracks cross the road.<br><br>ⓘ Trains could be approaching so look both ways and be prepared to stop. | |

5.  a) No bicycles allowed.
    b) This is a bicycle route.
    c) School zone ahead.
    d) Do not watch for bicycles.

    ℹ️ For everyone's safety bicycles are not allowed.

6.  a) No parking anytime.
    b) Parking only allowed for longer than 30 minutes, 9 a.m.–6 p.m.
    c) You can only park after 5:00 p.m.
    d) Parking allowed for a maximum of 30 minutes within times posted.

    ℹ️ This sign is usually in pairs or groups marking which areas you can park in.

7.  a) Turn right only on a red light.
    b) No right turn ever.
    c) No right turn allowed on a red light.
    d) Do not enter.

    ℹ️ If the traffic light is red at the intersection you may not turn right.

8.  a) Enter.
    b) Do not enter road.
    c) Come to a complete stop.
    d) Only bicycles allowed.

    ℹ️ Do not enter under any circumstance.

9. a) No wheelchair ramp.
   b) No parking at any time unless vehicle has a valid Accessible Parking Permit.
   c) No stopping at any time unless vehicle has a valid Accessible Parking Permit.
   d) No parking at any time.

   ⓘ You can only park in this area if your vehicle displays a valid Accessible Parking Permit.

10. a) Curb area reserved for picking up and dropping off people with disabilities.
    b) Curb area reserved for loading and unloading all passengers.
    c) Curb area reserved for vehicles parking with a valid permit.
    d) Curb area parking for all vehicles after 6:00 p.m.

    ⓘ Vehicles must display a valid Accessible Parking Permit in order to stop to load and unload people with disabilities.

11. a) No stopping.
    b) No parking.
    c) You may stand in the area between the signs.
    d) Bus stop is to the right and left.

    ⓘ Stopping is only allowed if loading or unloading passengers. This sign is used in groups or pairs.

12. a) No left turn.
    b) You may go in the opposite direction.
    c) No U-turn.
    d) Turning allowed after 6:00 p.m.

    ⓘ Do not turn around and go in the opposite direction.

13.  a) No stopping except to unload passengers.
     b) There is a stop sign ahead.
     c) Come to a complete stop.
     d) No stopping at any time between the signs.

ℹ️ Besides no stopping, you are not allowed to load or unload passengers between signs that look like this.

14.  a) No left turn during days and times posted.
     b) No left turn ever.
     c) Left turn allowed after 5:00 p.m.
     d) No left turn on Saturday or Sunday.

ℹ️ Carefully read the date and time as there is no left turn during days and times posted.

15.  a) Parking allowed on either side of the signs.
     b) Parking available after 6:00 p.m.
     c) No parking allowed between the signs.
     d) There is parking available on either side of the arrows.

ℹ️ When used in pairs, there is no parking between the signs unless you are loading or unloading people or merchandise.

16.  a) You are allowed to go straight through the intersection.
     b) You are not allowed to go straight through the intersection.
     c) You are not allowed to turn right or left.
     d) Stop at the intersection ahead.

ℹ️ You are not allowed to drive through the intersection so be prepared to turn.

17. a) You are approaching a school bus loading zone.
    b) Reduce speed to 40 km/h at all times.
    c) Reduce speed to 40 km/h when lights are flashing in this school zone.
    d) Watch for pedestrians at the crosswalk.

ℹ The speed is lower during school hours when the yellow lights are flashing. School sign may be neon yellow or blue.

18. a) You are approaching a school zone crosswalk.
    b) You are entering a school zone.
    c) All vehicles must stop on the side of the road where the school bus is.
    d) All vehicles must stop for a school bus in all directions when lights are flashing.

ℹ This sign is for multi-lane highways when there is no centre median divider.

19. a) There is an intersection ahead on the right.
    b) Stay to the left of the island.
    c) Stay to the right of the island.
    d) The road curves to the left for 1 km.

ℹ There is a traffic island ahead and you must keep to the right of it.

20. a) The speed limit is 50 km/h.
    b) The speed limit is 50 km/h ahead.
    c) It is 50 km to the next rest area.
    d) The speed limit is 50 km/h for a distance of 50 km.

ℹ The speed limit ahead is changing from what it is to 50 km/h.

21. a) Reduce speed ahead.
    b) Exit to the right.
    c) One-way traffic in the direction indicated by the arrow.
    d) Two-way traffic permitted.

ⓘ You can only travel in the direction of the arrow.

22. a) No pedestrians allowed on roadway.
    b) Pedestrians may not cross the road.
    c) There is no crosswalk in the area.
    d) Do not enter—construction zone.

ⓘ Pedestrians are not allowed on the road.

23. a) No passing on this road.
    b) You may pass on this road.
    c) Two-way traffic ahead.
    d) Do not enter.

ⓘ For safety reasons there is no passing on this roadway.

24. a) Right turn and passing lane ahead.
    b) Keep to the right except when passing on two-way road sections.
    c) Road turns to the right.
    d) Merge ahead.

ⓘ You are permitted to pass on the left; otherwise, keep to the right.

## Traffic Signs

25. a) Stop and yield right-of-way to pedestrians at crosswalk.  Do not pass from sign to crossing.
    b) Railroad crossing ahead, no pedestrians allowed.
    c) Pedestrians or vehicles may not enter the roadway.
    d) Deer crossing ahead.

    ⓘ You are approaching a pedestrian crosswalk. Slow down, yield to pedestrians and be prepared to stop.

26. a) If you are in lanes 1, 2 or 3 you must only go in the direction of that lane's arrow.
    b) If you are in lane 1 you may go straight and left.
    c) If you are in lane 2 you may go in any direction.
    d) If you are in lane 3, you may go straight or turn right.

    ⓘ These signs are either painted on the roadway or hung above at intersections. They tell drivers the direction they must travel for the lane they are in.

27. a) Lane is not for left turns.
    b) Lane is only for two-way left turns.
    c) Turn left or right.
    d) No U-turn.

    ⓘ This sign can be above the ground or on the road which means two-way left turns only.

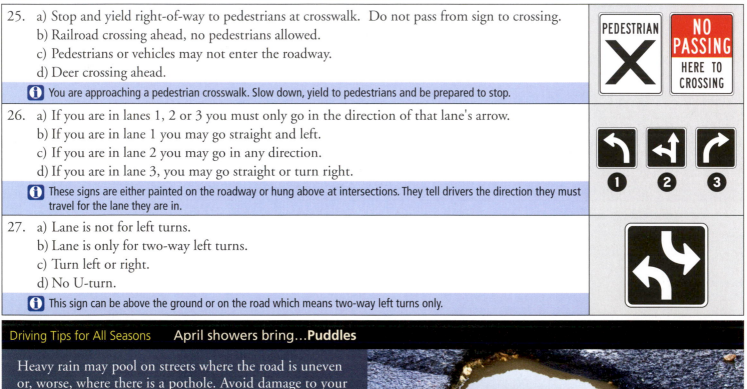

Driving Tips for All Seasons     April showers bring...**Puddles**

Heavy rain may pool on streets where the road is uneven or, worse, where there is a pothole. Avoid damage to your vehicle by slowing down in and around puddles.

# High Occupancy Vehicle (HOV) Signs

28. a) Lanes are for pedestrians only, no vehicles permitted during days and times posted.
    b) Lanes are for loading and unloading passengers only during days and times posted.
    c) Lanes are for 5 or more passengers during days and times posted.
    d) Lanes are for 3 or more passengers in the vehicles shown, plus bicycles, during the days and times shown or all the time (depending on the sign).

ⓘ These lanes are for bicycles or specific vehicles that carry 3 or more people, for the times indicated or all the time if no time is shown.

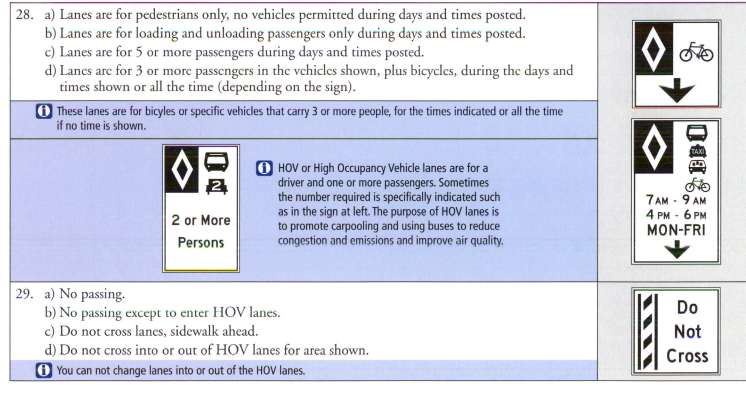

ⓘ HOV or High Occupancy Vehicle lanes are for a driver and one or more passengers. Sometimes the number required is specifically indicated such as in the sign at left. The purpose of HOV lanes is to promote carpooling and using buses to reduce congestion and emissions and improve air quality.

29. a) No passing.
    b) No passing except to enter HOV lanes.
    c) Do not cross lanes, sidewalk ahead.
    d) Do not cross into or out of HOV lanes for area shown.

ⓘ You can not change lanes into or out of the HOV lanes.

30. a) Crosswalk ahead, watch for pedestrians crossing.
    b) Intersection ahead, direction of arrow indicates who has right-of-way.
    c) Railroad crossing ahead.
    d) Quiet, church zone ahead.

    ⓘ When approaching an intersection with this sign the direction of the arrow indicates who has right-of-way.

31. a) Hidden left turn ahead.
    b) Hidden crosswalk ahead.
    c) There is a three-way stop ahead that is hidden.
    d) There is a hidden road ahead.

    ⓘ Drivers on the hidden road ahead may not see traffic from the main road when they reach the intersection.

32. a) The road narrows ahead.
    b) The two-way road curves ahead.
    c) A narrow bridge ahead.
    d) Slower traffic move to the right.

    ⓘ This symbol represents a bridge and that the bridge is narrower than the roadway.

33. a) There is a narrow bridge ahead.
    b) The road narrows ahead.
    c) Two-lane roadway ends.
    d) Merge with oncoming traffic.

    ⓘ The pavement will become narrower ahead.

34.  a) The road bends to the right ahead.
     b) The road bends to the left ahead.
     c) One-way traffic ahead.
     d) Right-turn-only lane ahead.
     (i) Adjust driving accordingly as the road bends or curves slightly to the right.

35.  a) One lane ahead.
     b) No turns ahead.
     c) The road branches off ahead.
     d) There is a three-way stop ahead.
     (i) The road divides ahead. Slow down in case you or others have to turn off the main roadway.

36.  a) Exit to the right.
     b) Sharp turn here.
     c) Crosswalk ahead.
     d) Railway crossing.
     (i) These arrowheads are called chevrons. They warn you about sharp turns and are posted in groups to guide drivers.

37.  a) Winding road ahead.
     b) Hidden intersection ahead.
     c) Turn right at bridge ahead.
     d) Road turns or bends to the right sharply ahead.
     (i) The road changes and bends sharply so reduce speed in order to follow the roadway safely.

| | |
|---|---|
| 38. a) Intersection ahead.<br>b) Stop sign ahead.<br>c) Stop at crosswalk ahead.<br>d) School children crossing ahead.<br><br>ⓘ There is a stop sign ahead so slow down. | |
| 39. a) Truck weigh station ahead.<br>b) Sharp turn ahead.<br>c) Hazard close to edge of road.<br>d) Single lane ahead.<br><br>ⓘ An island or something close to the road is a hazard. Downward lines indicate side to pass hazard on. | |
| 40. a) Slower traffic keep to the right.<br>b) Highway ends ahead.<br>c) The two-way road ahead is split with a median.<br>d) Merge with traffic ahead.<br><br>ⓘ The two-way road ahead will be split with a median. Each side of the road is one-way traffic. | |
| 41. a) Bridge ahead.<br>b) Gravel road ahead.<br>c) The two-way road ahead is not divided with a median.<br>d) The two-way road ahead is divided with a median.<br><br>ⓘ You will be required to share the road ahead with oncoming traffic. The road will not be divided by a median. | |

| 42. | a) A winding road is ahead.<br>b) Sharp turn in the road ahead.<br>c) Hazard to the right.<br>d) Hazard to the left. | |
|---|---|---|
| | ⓘ The road is winding ahead which may obstruct your ability to see other vehicles. | |
| 43. | a) Bridge ices.<br>b) Slippery when wet.<br>c) You are entering a snowbelt area.<br>d) Winding road ahead. | |
| | ⓘ The road is slippery when wet. Reduce speed and drive with caution. | |
| 44. | a) Road has a bend to the right.<br>b) Road turns sharply to the right.<br>c) Left lane ends ahead.<br>d) Right lane ends ahead. | |
| | ⓘ The right lane ends ahead and you are required to merge with traffic in the lane to the left if you are in the right lane. | |
| 45. | a) No bicycles allowed.<br>b) Official bicycle route.<br>c) School zone ahead.<br>d) Bicycle crossing ahead. | |
| | ⓘ Bicycle crossing ahead so slow down and proceed with caution. | |

46. a) Broken bridge ahead.
    b) Bridge ices ahead.
    c) Bridge lifts ahead to let boats pass.
    d) Do not drive on bridge ahead.

    ⓘ The bridge ahead will lift or swing up to let boats pass.

47. a) Paved road ends ahead.
    b) Gravel road ends ahead.
    c) One-way road ahead.
    d) Road ends ahead.

    ⓘ The paved road ends ahead and is replaced by a gravel road. Reduce speed accordingly.

48. a) Hidden intersection ahead.
    b) Two-lane highway begins.
    c) Two lanes will merge to one. Driver on the right has right-of-way.
    d) Two lanes will merge to one. Drivers in both lanes are responsible to merge safely.

    ⓘ Two lanes are merging into one. Merging is the equal responsibility of drivers in both lanes.

49. a) Divided highway begins.
    b) Divided highway ends.
    c) Slower traffic keep to the right.
    d) No intersection ahead.

    ⓘ Traffic goes in both directions ahead so stay on the right.

50. a) Snowmobiles cross this roadway.
    b) Only snowmobiles allowed in area.
    c) Provincial park area.
    d) Snowmobiles may not enter.

ⓘ Snowmobiles cross this area so drive cautiously as you may not see them.

51. a) Warning—construction zone ahead.
    b) Sharp turn ahead in the direction of the arrow.
    c) Road is very bumpy ahead.
    d) Road closed ahead.

ⓘ The checkered board pattern warns of danger so slow down and proceed with caution in the direction of the arrow.

52. a) No animals allowed.
    b) Deer may cross the road.
    c) You are entering a game farm.
    d) Watch for deer hunters.

ⓘ Deer may cross the road in this area. Slow down and be aware of your surroundings.

53. a) Construction zone ahead.
    b) Railroad crossing ahead.
    c) Traffic lights ahead.
    d) City zone ahead.

ⓘ You will be approaching a traffic light ahead. Slow down as you may have to stop.

54. a) There is a steep hill ahead.
    b) You are in a mountain zone.
    c) Caution, trucks turning.
    d) Construction zone ahead.

    ℹ️ The road has a steep hill ahead. Slow down and be prepared to shift into a lower gear to slow down your vehicle.

55. a) Trucks may approach the road from the right.
    b) Trucks may approach the road from the left.
    c) Construction zone.
    d) No trucks allowed on road.

    ℹ️ Truck entrance is on the side of the road where truck is shown, in this case on the right.

56. a) The road ends in 3.9 km.
    b) Only vehicles over 3.9 m permitted ahead.
    c) There is a maximum 3.9 m clearance ahead on the overpass.
    d) Divided highway ends in 3.9 km.

    ℹ️ If driving a tall vehicle you may not be able to pass. Take note of clearances before approaching underpasses.

57. a) Men at work ahead.
    b) Pedestrian crossing ahead.
    c) School zone ahead.
    d) Share the road with pedestrians.

    ℹ️ Watch for pedestrians as the roadway is meant to be shared. Drive cautiously.

58.  a) Watch out for fallen rocks.
     b) Steep hill, shift into lower gear.
     c) Construction zone ahead.
     d) Large hail stone area.
     ℹ️ Rocks could be falling so drive carefully and be prepared to avoid a collision.

59.  a) Railroad tracks ahead.
     b) Hospital ahead, keep quiet and watch for ambulances.
     c) School crossing ahead.
     d) You are approaching a hidden school bus stop.
     ℹ️ Be very cautious, watch for children and be prepared to stop for a school bus with flashing red lights.

60.  a) School crossing or school crossing ahead.
     b) Hidden school bus stop ahead.
     c) Children must be accompanied by an adult in this area.
     d) Intersection ahead.
     ℹ️ Watch for children crossing and follow the direction of the crossing guard. These signs may be neon yellow or blue.

61.  a) There is winding road for 50 km.
     b) Maximum safe speed to drive on ramp is 50 km/h.
     c) Drive at least 50 km on ramp.
     d) Next rest stop is in 50 km.
     ℹ️ All ramps have a maximum safe speed you can travel. Obey these maximums.

| | |
|---|---|
| 62. a) Bridge ahead.<br>b) Bridge ices.<br>c) Road may have water flowing over it.<br>d) Road ends at lake.<br>ⓘ Some roads are near high water areas where the road may get covered with water. Reduce speed and drive carefully. | |
| 63. a) Mountain zone ahead.<br>b) Bumpy or uneven road ahead.<br>c) Construction zone ahead.<br>d) Falling rocks ahead.<br>ⓘ Slow down and keep both hands on the steering wheel for best control of your vehicle and to avoid sudden shifts. | |
| 64. a) Survey crew working on road.<br>b) Road closed ahead.<br>c) 1 km construction zone begins.<br>d) Construction zone begins in 1 km.<br>ⓘ Road speed, curve and terrain may change in construction zone ahead. Slow down and drive cautiously. | |
| 65. a) Person controlling traffic ahead.<br>b) Roadwork ahead.<br>c) Survey crew assessing road ahead.<br>d) Construction zone ahead.<br>ⓘ Slow down and pay attention to instructions from the traffic control person ahead. | |

66. a) Movie filming set.
    b) Sightseeing binoculars ahead.
    c) Survey crew ahead.
    d) Bird watchers ahead.

ⓘ Surveyors often have to measure land in new areas. Use caution as surveyors may be near the road.

67. a) Fallen rock ahead.
    b) Snow removal ahead.
    c) Road work occurring ahead.
    d) Sand quarry ahead.

ⓘ Reduce speed, drive with caution and watch for construction personnel working on the road ahead.

68. a) There is a temporary detour from the normal traffic roadway.
    b) Be prepared to drive around mountains ahead.
    c) Downward sloping hill ahead.
    d) Closed lane ahead.

ⓘ The road detours temporarily from what it usually is due to road work.

69. a) Reduce speed. You are entering the construction zone.
    b) Construction zone begins in 1 km.
    c) Worker ahead surveying the land.
    d) Gravel road ahead.

ⓘ It is very important to obey the posted speed limits in construction zones as fines may be doubled.

| | |
|---|---|
| 70. a) Golf course ahead.<br>b) Fallen rocks ahead.<br>c) Provincial camp ground ahead.<br>d) There are grooves in the pavement.<br><br>ⓘ The pavement has been grooved so you may not be able to stop easily. Obey all posted speed limits for this area. | |
| 71. a) Right turn lane only ahead.<br>b) Lane is closed. Move into lane directed by arrow and merge with traffic.<br>c) Lane is open. Adjust speed for construction zone.<br>d) Hidden intersection ahead on right.<br><br>ⓘ Reduce your speed when merging with traffic in the lane shown by the arrow. | |
| 72. a) Bridge narrows ahead.<br>b) Bridge ahead.<br>c) Third lane begins.<br>d) Lane ends and is closed for roadwork.<br><br>ⓘ Lane ahead is closed and you must merge with traffic in the lane that is open. Obey all posted speed limits. | |
| 73. a) Winding road ahead.<br>b) Follow the road in the direction shown.<br>c) Watch for farm vehicles approaching from the left.<br>d) Construction zone begins to the left.<br><br>ⓘ Always follow the arrows with flashing lights as they indicate which direction to follow. | |

74. a) Stop and drive slowly through campground.
    b) Obey the crossing guard with the signs they hold up.
    c) Slow down and be prepared to stop.
    d) Slow down, stop and exit the construction zone.

ⓘ These signs may be held by road work personnel. Drive slowly and be prepared to stop.

75. a) Pass the pace vehicle only when you see this sign flashing.
    b) Do not pass the pace vehicle that has this sign flashing.
    c) Pass only to the left.
    d) Pass only to the right.

ⓘ Do not pass vehicles with this flashing sign.

76. a) The road detours so follow this sign until you come to the regular road.
    b) Follow the detour marker only if you choose not to take the regular road.
    c) Merge with road that closed.
    d) Lane closed ahead. Slow down and merge with traffic.

ⓘ Follow this sign through the detour until you come to the regular road.

**Driving Tips for All Seasons**    **Stay hydrated**

Keep cool water with you when travelling on hot summer days, even for short distances. Construction, which is very common in summer, can delay you considerably. Do not let yourself dehydrate.

77.  a) An exit sign telling you which lane to drive in if you want to exit to Bradley Street.
     b) Two right lanes must exit to Bradley Street.
     c) Only the right lane exits to Bradley Street.
     d) No left turns on Bradley Street.

ℹ️ Exit signs indicate which lane to drive in if you want to exit or if you want to stay on the main road.

78.  a) A highway exit is coming up in 20 km.
     b) A highway exit is coming up in 10 km.
     c) An advance exit sign telling you which lanes go off the highway.
     d) An advance exit sign telling you 2 right lanes do not exit off the highway.

ℹ️ Advance signs are also used with exit signs. Ensure you are in the correct lane to exit a highway.

79.  a) Indicates which direction to go for the city or town posted.
     b) All towns or cities posted on this sign are 50 km away.
     c) Construction ahead so be prepared to detour by direction shown.
     d) Indicates there is provincial park in the city or town posted.

ℹ️ This direction and information sign tells you which direction to travel to get to the city or town posted.

80.  a) Indicates which direction to go for the city or town posted.
     b) Indicates distance, in kilometres, to the city or town posted.
     c) Indicates the distance to campgrounds and green conservation areas.
     d) Indicates by distance shown that Guelph is before Hamilton.

ℹ️ Sign tells you the distance, in kilometres, from the city or town posted. Helps with rest stops and gas planning.

81.   a) One left lane exits off the highway.
     b) Two left lanes exit off the highway.
     c) Right lane only exits off the highway.
     d) One or more lanes allow you to exit off the highway.

ⓘ Advance signs indicate which lanes exit off the highway, by the yellow boxed "exit" notation.

82.   a) To get to the Q.E.W. go by way of the 403.
     b) Both the Q.E.W. and the 401 are coming up on the right.
     c) The Q.E.W. is coming up on the right.
     d) The 401 is coming up on the right.

ⓘ Highways are connected and in this case you get to the Q.E.W. by way of (via) the 403.

83.   a) Interchange 346 is 346 km from Toronto.
     b) It is 34.6 km to Dixie Rd.
     c) You will be approaching interchange 346 in 1 km.
     d) You will be approaching the Dixie Rd. exit in 346 km.

ⓘ Highway 401 begins in Windsor so interchange 346, Dixie Rd., is 346 km from Windsor.

84.   a) Traffic bulletin signs change with updates on traffic, delays and lane closures.
     b) Traffic bulletin signs post the same information on traffic, delays and lane closures.
     c) Informs drivers about next exits.
     d) Informs drivers about nearby parks and recreation information.

ⓘ These signs inform drivers about current driving conditions so that alternate routes can be taken.

85. a) Airplane parking area.
    b) Route to airport.
    c) Route to airplane production.
    d) Indicates you are under a fly zone.

    ℹ️ Follow these signs to get to an airport.

86. a) Boat docking route.
    b) Deep water ahead.
    c) Ferry service route.
    d) No public swimming ahead.

    ℹ️ Follow these signs to get to a ferry service.

87. a) Indicates there are police, a hospital, an information desk and an airport in one building.
    b) Indicates there is only an airport nearby.
    c) Shows what services and facilities are not available nearby or off-road.
    d) Shows what services and facilities are located nearby or off-road.

    ℹ️ Indicates what services and facilities are available off the road. Other services can include car pool lots, universities, etc.

88. a) Wheelchair parking only.
    b) Indicates facilities accessible by wheelchair.
    c) Indicates retirement living community. Slow down and keep noise low.
    d) Indicates there is a hospital nearby.

    ℹ️ Indicates there are ramps and other wheelchair accessible facilities.

89.  a) Railroad crossing ahead.
     b) Train maintenance area.
     c) Route to cargo railway station.
     d) Route to passenger railway station.

ℹ️ Indicates route to where passengers can be met or dropped off at the railway station.

90.  a) Speed in area is very slow, less than 40 km/h.
     b) Slow-moving vehicle on road, travelling less than 40 km/h.
     c) Snow removal vehicle ahead.
     d) Danger, keep out, road under construction.

ℹ️ All vehicles moving less than 40 km/hr must display a slow-moving vehicle sign at rear if driving on a road.

91.  a) Bilingual signs are for educational purposes only.
     b) Bilingual signs are posted near French schools for you to follow.
     c) Obey bilingual sign only if you read and speak French.
     d) Bilingual signs provide important information. Read message in language understood best.

ℹ️ Bilingual signs have two languages on one sign. Sometimes, there may be two signs, one English and one French.

92.  a) Two exits exist for Bowesville Road.
     b) Only exit onto Bowesville Road if you drive an emergency vehicle.
     c) Numbers at the bottom assist emergency vehicles to plan best routes.
     d) Some information signs have numbers at the bottom to assist you with exits and distances.

ℹ️ The numbering system at the bottom of some signs is to help emergency vehicles plan the best route.

**93. When are you required to wear a seatbelt?**

a) Wearing a seatbelt is optional.

b) Only drivers are required to wear a seatbelt.

c) Only passengers are required to wear a seatbelt.

d) All drivers and passengers are required to wear a seatbelt and be properly buckled up.

> ⓘ Drivers will receive a fine up to $1,000 and 2 demerit points for not wearing a seatbelt. Drivers must ensure all passengers under the age of 16 are properly buckled up. Unbuckled passengers 16 years and older can be fined.

**94. What does the law state about seatbelts and children 9–18 kg (20–40lbs)?**

a) All infants, toddlers and children under 8 must be in a booster seat.

b) All infants, toddlers and children under 8 must be in a rear-facing child car seat.

c) All infants, toddlers and children under 8 must wear protective head gear.

d) All toddlers 9–18 kg must be in an approved child car seat that is properly attached.

> ⓘ A child's weight and/or age determines what type of car seat is required. It is important that all child car seats meet safety standards and are properly secured.

**95. How far away must headlights and rear lights be seen?**

a) From 50 m away.

b) From 150 m away.

c) From 1150 m away.

d) They must be seen clearly in the dark.

> ⓘ You must also have your rear licence plate illuminated with white lighting when headlights are on. Ensure headlights are on 1/2 an hour before sunset and leave them on for 1/2 an hour after sunrise.

**96. When using highbeam lights when do you have to switch to lowbeam lights?**

a) Within 150 m of oncoming vehicles.

b) Within 50 m of oncoming vehicles.

c) You do not have to switch.

d) If the oncoming car puts their highbeams on you do not have to switch.

ⓘ Use lowbeam lights when you are less than 60 m behind another vehicle and within 150 m of oncoming vehicles. Never use parking lights for driving. They are only for parking.

**97. Why must your vehicle undergo emissions testing?**

a) To identify if it's grossly polluting the environment.

b) Your vehicle may be of an age where it's necessary to get tested.

c) So that you may renew your vehicle registration.

d) All of the above.

ⓘ If you receive notice to get emissions testing, your car must pass in order to get a renewal sticker so that you may drive your vehicle.

**98. Why must you use signals when turning?**

a) To inform other drivers of what you want to do.

b) To inform pedestrians of what you want to do.

c) To send out an alert of your intentions.

d) All of the above.

ⓘ Failing to use proper signals can result in a fine and demerit points. Always signal to inform others of your intention. Follow all rules for turning.

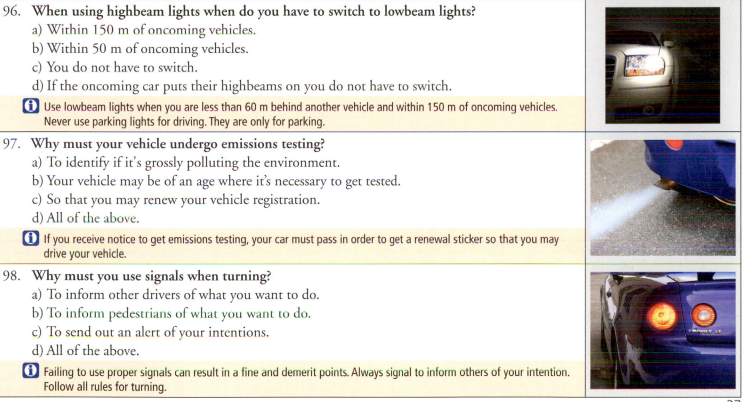

**99. Unless posted in cities, towns, villages and built-up areas the maximum speed limit is?…**

a) 40 km/h.

b) 50 km/h.

c) 70 km/h.

d) 80 km/h.

ⓘ Where no speed limit is posted, the limit is 80 km/h outside these areas.

**100. What are you required to do if a police officer signals you to pull over?**

a) Slow down, safely pull over in the left lane and come to a complete stop.

b) Slow down, safely pull over in the right lane and come to a complete stop.

c) Slow down and stop in the lane you are in.

d) Signal and stop at the next intersection and wait for the police officer.

ⓘ Do not get out of your vehicle. Wait for the police officer to come to you.

**101. How much time do you have to surrender your licence, vehicle permit (or copy) and insurance when asked by a police officer?**

a) Immediately.

b) Within 12 hours.

c) Within 24 hours.

d) You do not have to, they will look you up in the system.

ⓘ You must present these required documents immediately. Failure to do so can result in a fine.

102. **How much space should you have between you and any vehicle you are following?**
   a) No rule applies and you will not get a fine or demerit points as long as caution is used.
   b) There is a rule of 20 seconds but it is for motorcycle drivers only.
   c) At least 12 seconds so you can see around the vehicle ahead and also have enough time to stop.
   d) At least 2 seconds so you can see around the vehicle ahead and also have enough time to stop.

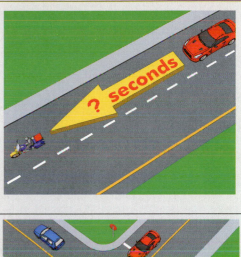

 If driving conditions are not ideal add more space especially if driving in bad weather or following larger vehicles, motorcycles, or when you have a heavy load. Use markers on the road to help determine correct following distance.

103. **If 3 vehicles are at an all-way stop, who has the right-of-way?**
   a) The vehicle that got there first.
   b) The vehicle on the left.
   c) The vehicle turning right.
   d) The vehicle turning left.

Always yield the right-of-way to the vehicle that came to the stop first.

104. **If 2 vehicles come to an uncontrolled intersection at the same time, who has the right-of-way?**

    a) The vehicle on the right.

    b) The vehicle on the left.

    c) The vehicle turning right.

    d) The vehicle turning left.

ⓘ The driver on the left must let the driver on the right go first at intersections with no signs or lights.

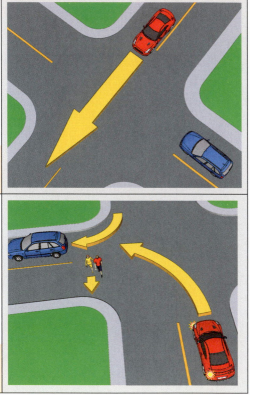

105. **If you are turning left at an uncontrolled intersection and a pedestrian is crossing your path, who has the right-of-way?**

    a) You do. Come to a complete stop and make your turn.

    b) Any other car at the intersection that is turning right.

    c) You must yield the right-of-way to approaching traffic and/or to pedestrians crossing.

    d) Whoever is more in a hurry goes first.

ⓘ Always yield the right-of-way to pedestrians no matter the direction you are turning.

106. **If you approach an intersection on a main road that is blocked with traffic, what should you do?**
   a) Stop before entering the intersection.
   b) Move up so cars behind you can move forward.
   c) Slowly proceed through the intersection.
   d) Turn left or right to avoid the heavy traffic back-up.

ℹ️ Only proceed after stopping and when the way is clear. Do not allow yourself to be stuck in the intersection as the light turns red.

107. **How much room do cyclists need on either side of themselves as a safety zone?**
   a) 4 m.
   b) 3 m.
   c) 2 m.
   d) 1 m.

ℹ️ Failing to leave the required amount of space could result in a fine and 2 demerit points and jeopardize the safety of the cyclist.

108. **What challenges do commercial vehicles have that are dangerous for other vehicles?**
    a) They have small blind spots.
    b) They make wide turns.
    c) They roll forward after stopping.
    d) They block large amounts of snow and slush from your windshield.

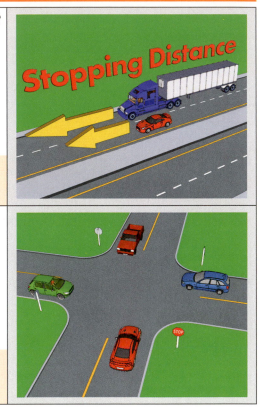

ℹ️ Always leave enough road space around large commercial vehicles. Be aware of what they can and cannot do.

109. **Coming to a complete stop at an intersection is required, but where do you stop if there is no stop line, crosswalk or sidewalk?**
    a) You stop right beside the stop sign.
    b) You stop right before the stop sign.
    c) You stop at the edge of the intersection.
    d) You stop a little into the intersection so that you can see traffic and pedestrians.

ℹ️ You must also wait for the intersection to clear before entering it.

110. **When do you stop for school buses if there is a median?**
   a) Whenever you approach and see one.
   b) Never, because they will stop for you.
   c) Whenever they stop.
   d) Only if you are behind a stopped bus which has its upper red alternating lights flashing.

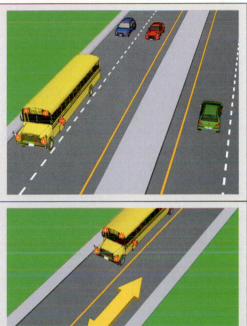

ⓘ School buses also have flashing stop signs that swing out from the driver's side, notifying vehicles to stop. Stay back the required distance.

111. **If there is no median, how far in front and behind a school bus are you required to stop when its lights are flashing?**
   a) At least 20 m behind and far enough in front for children to exit the bus and cross safely.
   b) At least 20 ft behind and far enough in front for children to exit the bus and cross safely.
   c) At least 10 m behind and far enough in front for children to exit the bus and cross safely.
   d) At least 10 ft behind and far enough in front for children to exit the bus and cross safely.

ⓘ Only proceed when the bus lights have stopped flashing or the bus has moved.

112. **When you come to a railway crossing and there are flashing signal lights, what must you do?**
    a) Continue slowly because flashing lights are only a warning to drive slow.
    b) Stop and then proceed slowly across the tracks.
    c) Stop and wait for the signal lights to stop flashing.
    d) Drive around the gate or barrier to avoid getting stuck on the tracks.

    ℹ Stop at least 5 m back from the nearest rail, gate or barrier. Only cross tracks once gates rise and lights stop flashing.

113. **It is illegal to not stop behind a stopped school bus with alternating flashing red lights. If you do not stop what can happen on a first offence?**
    a) You can be fined $40–$200 and get 2 demerit points.
    b) You can be fined $400–$2,000 and get 6 demerit points.
    c) You can be fined $4,000–$20,000.
    d) You will not be fined for the first offence; you will only receive a warning.

    ℹ You can get 6 demerit points for a first offence and a fine of $400–$2,000.

114. **You must share the road with motorcycles, cyclists, commercial vehicles, pedestrians, farm machinery and buses.**
    a) The above statement is false.
    b) The above statement is true.
    c) All of the above are correct except for farm machinery.
    d) All of the above are correct except for pedestrians because they are not in a vehicle.

    ℹ You must share the road with all vehicles and pedestrians. Failing to do so can result in a fine and demerit points.

**115.** **Can you make a right turn on a red light?**

a) Yes, after coming to a complete stop and as long as a sign does not tell you otherwise.

b) Yes, as long as you are in an HOV lane.

c) No, there are no right turns on red lights allowed in Ontario.

d) No, there are no right turns on roadways shared with pedestrians.

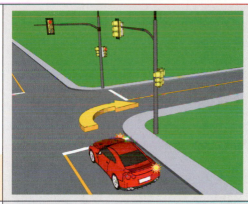

ⓘ Ensure you first come to a complete stop and that your way is clear before making your turn.

**116.** **How do you make a left turn from a two-way road onto a two-way road?**

a) Turn from the right lane making a smooth arc into the right curb lane.

b) Turn from the right lane making a smooth arc into the lane right of the centre line.

c) Turn from the closest lane to the centre dividing line into the right curb lane.

d) Turn from the closest lane to the centre dividing line making a smooth arc into the lane to the right of the centre dividing line.

ⓘ Unless otherwise posted left turns are made from the far left lane. Signal, check all directions and ensure way is clear. After turning move into the right curb lane when it is clear to do so.

117. **How do you make a left turn from a two-way road onto a two lane one-way road?**
    a) Turn from the far left lane into the left curb lane.
    b) Turn from the far left lane into the right curb lane.
    c) Turn from the far right lane into the left curb lane.
    d) Turn from the right lane into the right curb lane.

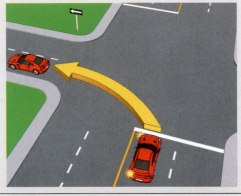

ℹ️ Always signal in advance, check all directions and then proceed slowly making a smooth arc.

118. **Why is it a bad idea to turn your steering wheel to the left while waiting to make a left turn at an intersection?**
    a) In case you need to turn right—it will be harder to steer out of the turn.
    b) It is not a bad idea—your vehicle will not be able to make the turn in time if you do not.
    c) Another vehicle can push your vehicle into oncoming traffic.
    d) Turning your steering wheel unnecessarily will add to your car's wear and tear.

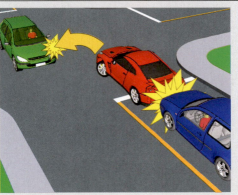

ℹ️ Only turn your steering wheel to the left when you can make the turn.

119. **What do the markings on the road mean and what does the sign represent in the picture?**
    a) There is a left turn lane in the centre for those travelling north.
    b) There is a left turn lane in the centre for those travelling south.
    c) There is an extra lane for driving in.
    d) There is a two-way left turn lane in the centre for traffic going in both directions.

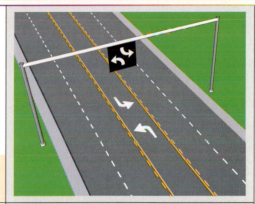

ℹ️ Signal and move into the left turn lane. Make your turn carefully and only when the way is clear.

120. **Can you turn left on a red light from a one-way road onto a one-way road?**
    a) Yes, if you signal, stop first in the farthest left lane and then proceed when the way is clear.
    b) Yes, as long as you drive slowly and cautiously.
    c) No left turns are permitted on a red light in Ontario.
    d) Left turns are only permitted from two-way roads to two-way roads on a green light.

ℹ️ Ensure you yield to pedestrians and traffic after first coming to a complete stop.

**121. To make a U-turn you must be able to see how far in both directions?**

  a) 50 m.

  b) 100 m.

  c) 150 m.

  d) 200 m.

ⓘ Never make a U-turn on a curve, hill, railway crossing, bridge, tunnel or where your view is blocked. It is illegal to do so.

**122. When can you remove your seatbelt while driving?**

  a) When you are backing up.

  b) When you are the only person in the car.

  c) If you are a G1 driver.

  d) If you are on a country road.

ⓘ To see properly while backing up you can remove your seatbelt to turn your body. Remember to put it back on as soon as you move forward.

**123. When parking uphill with a curb what should you do?**

  a) Turn your tires to the left to catch the curb if your vehicle rolls backward.

  b) Turn your tires to the right to catch the curb if your vehicle rolls backward.

  c) Make your tires straight and parallel with the curb.

  d) The direction of your tires does not matter as long as you set the parking brake.

ⓘ Turn your tires to the left and set your parking brake. Always do both.

**124. Who has the right-of-way in a roundabout?**
   a) Traffic approaching the roundabout.
   b) Traffic in the roundabout.
   c) Traffic turning right in the roundabout.
   d) Traffic turning left in the roundabout.

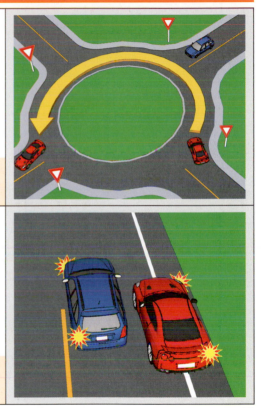

ℹ️ Slow down when approaching the yield line at roundabouts. Only stop at yield line if necessary. Enter when clear and travel with traffic flow in a counter-clockwise direction.

**125. When can you pass on a shoulder?**
   a) Only if a vehicle is turning left and you have an unpaved shoulder on the right.
   b) Only if a vehicle is turning left and you have a paved shoulder on the right.
   c) Whenever the vehicle in front of you is moving under 40 km/h.
   d) Whenever you can do so safely.

ℹ️ Passing is generally done from the left but you can pass on the right in this case if there is another vehicle turning left and only if the shoulder is paved.

126. **Two solid yellow painted lines on a roadway as in this diagram do which of the following?**
    a) Help in calculating distances from one exit to the next.
    b) Act as left and right turn lane markings.
    c) Provide drivers information about upcoming exits.
    d) Are warnings to guide drivers away from fixed obstacles like islands, bridges etc.

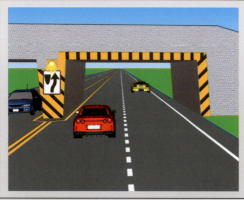

ⓘ Steer clear of solid painted road markings that are around fixed objects to avoid a collision.

127. **What do double solid pavement markings mean?**
    a) Vehicles travelling on the right may pass when the way is clear.
    b) Vehicles travelling on the left may pass when the way is clear.
    c) Both vehicles may pass in either direction when the way is clear.
    d) No vehicles may pass in either direction.

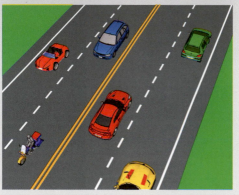

ⓘ Solid yellow lines divide traffic going in opposite directions and do not allow vehicles to pass in either direction.

**128. What must you do when changing lanes?**

a) Check mirrors and blind spots for space, signal, check for space again, steer into lane.

b) Signal and steer into lane slowly.

c) Signal and steer into lane quickly to get into lane safely.

d) Sound horn, signal and move slowly.

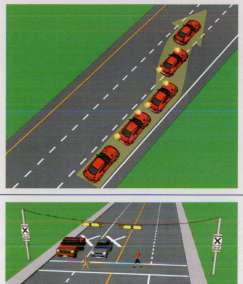

ℹ Checks and double checks as well as steering into the new lane at a gradual or slightly greater speed are necessary for proper and safe turns.

**129. What must drivers do at pedestrian crossovers and school crossings?**

a) Stop and wait until the lane you are in is clear.

b) Stop and wait until all pedestrians, including school crossing guards, have completely crossed the road.

c) Stop and wait until all pedestrians have almost crossed the road.

d) Slow down and proceed with caution.

ℹ Drivers who do not come to a complete stop and yield the entire roadway at pedestrian crossovers and school crossings where there is a crossing guard present displaying a school crossing stop sign will be fined up to $500 and get 3 demerit points.

**130. What are passing or climbing lanes for?**

    a) They allow for frequent stops and a rest area ahead.

    b) They are for vehicles that have trouble climbing hills.

    c) They help thin out traffic by providing an extra lane.

    d) They allow slower vehicles to move into the right lane so faster ones can pass on the left.

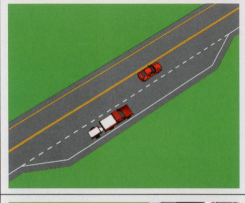

ℹ️ Advance notice of passing lanes is provided as are signs warning when these lanes end. If driving at a reduced speed, move into the right lane and allow faster moving vehicles to pass. Merge safely back when passing lane ends.

**131. When can you pass on the right?**

    a) You may never pass on the right.

    b) You can only pass on the right if there is an emergency.

    c) On one-way or multi-lane roads, when passing a streetcar or a vehicle turning left.

    d) On any type of road providing there is an unpaved shoulder.

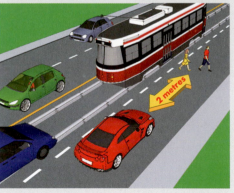

ℹ️ When passing a streetcar ensure passengers are not getting on or off. If they are, stay at least 2 m behind the back doors. If a safety island exists, drive cautiously and be on the look-out for pedestrians.

**132. Which one of these statements is a basic parking rule?**

a) Park on a curve or hill so that you can see ahead.

b) Do not park within 3 m of a fire hydrant.

c) Do not park within 150 m of intersections with traffic lights.

d) Do not look while opening your door.

ⓘ Park where you will not block other parked vehicles, sidewalks or roadways. Never park on a curve, near a crosswalk, fire hydrant or near an intersection. Be careful and watch for cyclists and pedestrians when opening your door.

**133. High Occupancy Vehicle lanes on provincial highways are reserved for vehicles carrying at least how many passengers?**

a) The driver plus 1 other passenger for a total of 2.

b) The driver plus 2 other passengers for a total of 3.

c) The driver plus 3 other passengers for a total of 4.

d) The driver plus 4 other passengers for a total of 5.

ⓘ Other roadways will specify the number required. Obey the number of passengers required or risk getting a fine and demerit points. HOV lanes provide many benefits, from reduced traffic to reduced vehicle emissions.

**? or More Persons**

**134. What should you do if you hit a deer or moose?**

a) Try to move the animal off the road so other vehicles will not hit it.

b) Sound your horn to ward off other animals from coming onto the roadway.

c) Report the incident to the Ministry of Natural Resources or local police.

d) Do nothing but drive cautiously as more animals may be in the area.

ⓘ Never try to move an injured animal as it may increase your chances of being hit by another vehicle.

**135. What should you do if you are the victim of road rage?**

    a) Lock the doors and remain in your vehicle.

    b) If you have a cell phone, safely pull over and call police.

    c) Attract attention to your car by honking the horn and using your signals.

    d) All of the above.

ℹ️ Be a polite and courteous driver. Never compete, retaliate or try to educate other drivers, which can lead to road rage.

**136. What should you do when approaching a construction zone?**

    a) Slow down as signs may be posted with reduced speed limits.

    b) Obey all warning signs.

    c) Follow the directions of the traffic control worker.

    d) All of the above.

ℹ️ Fines for speeding are doubled when workers are present in construction zones.

**137. What should you do if you feel drowsy while driving?**

    a) Reduce speed.

    b) Turn up your radio.

    c) Take a nap off the road in a safe area.

    d) Open all windows.

ℹ️ Drinking coffee or other measures to make you alert are not effective. Driving while drowsy is linked to many accidents so ensure you are well-rested and alert.

**138. Under what circumstances are cell phones not allowed while driving?**

    a) When you use your cell phone to text.

    b) When you use your hand-held cell phone to chat.

    c) When you use your cell phone to check and send emails.

    d) All of the above.

ⓘ Convicted drivers face fines and demerit points while a novice driver faces licence suspension and cancellation.

**139. What does the Accessible Parking Permit give you?**

    a) It gives everyone in your family the privilege to park, stand or stop in any area.

    b) Allows parking in designated spaces even if the person with the disability is not a passenger.

    c) Allows parking everywhere during specified times.

    d) Allows parking in designated spaces for you or passengers with you who qualified for the parking permit.

ⓘ The permit must belong to you or one of your passengers.

**140. When approaching a stopped emergency vehicle with its sirens or red lights flashing, or a towtruck with amber lights flashing you must?…**

    a) Slow down and drive cautiously. You must leave one lane clearance between you and an emergency vehicle if there are multiple lanes in your direction.

    b) Maintain the posted rate of speed for the area.

    c) Slow down, stop and pull over to the right.

    d) Slow down, stop and pull over to the left.

ⓘ For a first offence you can be fined $400–$2,000, get 3 demerit points and possible licence suspension.

141. **How can driver distractions be avoided?**
    a) Plan your trip in advance and know where you are going.
    b) Eat before driving to avoid the need to snack.
    c) Preset CD players, radios and other controls before driving.
    d) All of the above.

ℹ️ Avoid careless-driving charges and demerit points by avoiding all driving distractions.

142. **What should you do when glare from bright sunshine makes seeing difficult?**
    a) Wear a good pair of sunglasses that cut glare well.
    b) Use your sun visors and adjust them according to the glare.
    c) Reduce speed when entering a tunnel, remove sun glasses, turn on lowbeam headlights.
    d) All of the above.

ℹ️ If approaching vehicles at night with glaring headlights, look slightly to the right and above oncoming vehicles. Do not look right at the headlights. Take steps to reduce glare where possible.

143. **If driving in fog that becomes very dense, what should you do?**
    a) Carefully pass vehicles that are moving too slowly or following too closely.
    b) Pull off the road onto the shoulder and wait for the fog to clear.
    c) Turn on emergency flashers and pull off the road completely into a safe parking area.
    d) Slow down and turn on your fog lights.

ℹ️ Do not become the first vehicle hit in a chain reaction. Get off the road completely and keep emergency lights flashing. Wait until fog has lifted before driving.

144. **Which statement is false about driving in the rain?**
   a) Rain can reduce visibility.
   b) Rain can fill potholes and cause damage to your car.
   c) Rain can cause your vehicle to hydroplane (ride the water like skis).
   d) Rain can increase your braking ability.

   ⓘ Reduce speed in rain as roads become slippery, especially at the start when moisture mixes with oil and grease from the road surface.

145. **If you skid on a slippery road surface what should you do?**
   a) Steer your vehicle into the direction you want to go.
   b) Steer your vehicle into the opposite direction you want to go.
   c) Apply gas to quickly get out of the skid.
   d) Turn off the ignition.

   ⓘ Skids generally happen because a vehicle is travelling too fast for road, weather or traffic conditions. Always adapt driving accordingly.

146. **What is black ice?**
   a) When snow is mixed with mud and then freezes.
   b) When newly paved roads are wet.
   c) When asphalt has a thin layer of ice on it.
   d) When ice is mixed with snow.

   ⓘ Black ice can form anywhere, especially on bridges which get extra cold air from below. This causes the temperature to drop more quickly on the bridge forming a thin layer of ice.

**147. Snow may be as slippery as ice; what should you do when driving on snow-covered roads?**
   a) Look ahead and slow down.
   b) Avoid steering suddenly.
   c) Avoid braking suddenly.
   d) All of the above.

ⓘ When possible avoid driving in snow by checking weather forecasts regularly. If it is still necessary to drive, do so cautiously.

**148. What should you do if you encounter dangerous whiteout conditions?**
   a) Pass vehicles that are moving too slowly or following too closely.
   b) Pull onto the shoulder and wait for the conditions to change.
   c) Turn on emergency flashers and pull off the road completely into a safe parking area.
   d) Maintain speed and turn on your emergency flashers.

ⓘ Dangerous whiteout conditions can mean serious accidents. Do not risk your life or endanger others. Find a safe parking area and wait for conditions to improve.

**149. What vehicle has flashing blue lights that can be seen 150 m away?**
   a) A school bus.
   b) A tow truck.
   c) A snow removal vehicle.
   d) An ambulance.

ⓘ Snow removal vehicles are slow and can be wide. To clear highways there may be groups of them across the road. Do not try to speed around them.

150. **If driving and your brakes fail what should you do?**
    a) Turn off the ignition.
    b) Keep your foot on the brake and apply strong downward pressure.
    c) Pump the brakes to restore hydraulic brake pressure.
    d) Sound horn and steer to a clear area.

ⓘ Regular vehicle service with brake checking is the best way to avoid brake failure.

151. **What should you do if your gas pedal sticks?**
    a) First try to lift the pedal with your foot.
    b) First try to reach down and lift the pedal with your hands.
    c) Sound your horn to warn others of your problem.
    d) Drive onto a sidewalk.

ⓘ If lifting the pedal with your foot does not work, turn on your emergency lights, shift into neutral and gradually stop, ideally off the road.

152. **What should you do if your car is about to stall on the highway?**
    a) Honk your horn for help.
    b) Stop and put on your hazard lights.
    c) Pull over to the closest shoulder as quickly as possible.
    d) Continue at a reduced speed; you may not even have a problem.

ⓘ Pull over to the shoulder as carefully and quickly as possible by slowing down, checking all mirrors and putting on your emergency lights.

**153. What should you do if you have a tire blow-out?**
a) Step on the gas pedal and quickly move off the road.
b) Firmly steer into the safest direction and remove your foot from the gas pedal.
c) Stop and put on your hazard lights.
d) Honk your horn for help.

ⓘ Blow-outs at high speeds can be very dangerous. Remain calm, take your foot off the gas pedal and firmly steer where you want to go.

**154. If you are in an accident with no personal injuries and damages are $2,000 or less, you should?…**
a) Call 911 even if damages are less than $2,000.
b) Move driveable vehicles off the road to enable traffic to move freely, and exchange information.
c) Leave cars with damages where they are so that police can determine fault.
d) Call an ambulance in case someone hits your car and gets hurt.

ⓘ As long as no one is hurt and damages are less than $2,000, move driveable vehicles off the road safely to allow traffic to flow. Then call police services, not 911, and obtain the closest Collision Reporting Centre to report the accident.

**155. If you are in an accident with no personal injuries, but damages are over $2,000, you should?**
a) Exchange information with the other party and leave.
b) Call police and give them information about the accident and damages.
c) Leave the scene, as "no fault" insurance handles this.
d) All of the above.

ⓘ Provide as much information to police about the accident as possible giving them information about vehicles and damages. Also obtain witness contact information to give police.

156. **When involved in or witness to an accident where someone has been injured, you should?...**
  a) Call or have someone else call for help immediately.
  b) Turn off the vehicle and turn on the emergency lights.
  c) If you are not injured, stay calm and offer help until emergency services arrive.
  d) All of the above.

  ⓘ In case of a fuel leak ensure no one is smoking or lights a match. Call for help. Stay calm and cover accident victims with a blanket or jacket to reduce shock.

157. **If a police officer or inspector from the MTO deems your vehicle unsafe, what can happen?**
  a) Your vehicle can be taken off the road.
  b) Your licence plates can be removed and taken.
  c) You could receive a fine if you refuse the inspection.
  d) All of the above.

  ⓘ You must fix whatever problem is identified during an inspection by a police officer or inspector from the Ontario Ministry of Transportation (MTO) before you can put your vehicle safely and legally back on the road.

158. **When and how often do you have to renew your driver's licence?**
  a) Whenever you receive a renewal application in the mail and/or before your licence expires.
  b) You do not have to renew as you have already passed all required tests.
  c) Every 10 years.
  d) Every 20 years.

  ⓘ If you do not receive a renewal application or renewal postcard in the mail you are still responsible for ensuring you have a valid driver's licence that has not expired. Contact the Ministry of Transportation for further information.

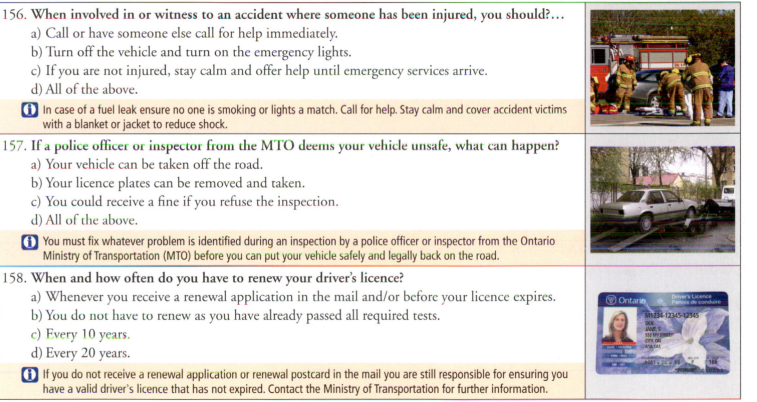

159. **If there are continuity lines to the right of your vehicle in the lane you are in what must you do?**

   a) You must turn into another lane as your lane is exiting or ending.

   b) You are not required to do anything unless you want to exit. Your lane is unaffected.

   c) You must merge with the traffic to your left.

   d) You must merge with the traffic to your right.

   ⓘ White lines closer together and wider than other white lines are continuity lines. Continuity lines to your left mean your lane is ending so you must turn or exit. Continuity lines to your right mean your lane is unaffected.

160. **On a vehicle's left side what does a broken yellow pavement marking beside a solid yellow line mean?**

   a) Cars travelling in the other direction may pass when the way is clear.

   b) You may pass when the way is clear.

   c) No cars may pass in either direction.

   d) Both cars may pass in either direction when the way is clear.

   ⓘ Broken yellow lines in the lane to your left mean you may pass when the way is clear. There may even be a solid yellow line to the left of that, meaning you may still pass when clear but vehicles in the opposite direction may not.

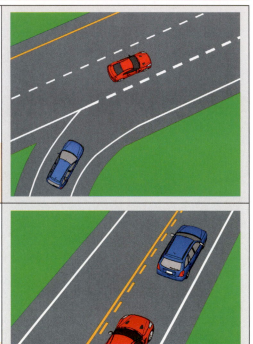

161. **If a traffic light is red, but there is a green arrow pointing left, what does that mean?**

   a) Vehicles in the left turning lane may turn left.

   b) Vehicles in the left turning lane may turn right.

   c) No vehicles may turn—only pedestrians may cross.

   d) The direction of the green arrow indicates there is a one-way street.

   ⓘ Vehicles in both directions may be turning left. If the arrow turns yellow, a green light will soon appear in one or more directions. Stop if you can safely; if not, complete a left turn cautiously.

162. **What does the round signal with a white vertical line on it represent in the picture?**

   a) It is a left turn signal.

   b) It is a spare light should the other ones malfunction.

   c) It is a symbol indicating pedestrians may not cross.

   d) It is a transit priority signal allowing public transit vehicles the right-of-way.

   ⓘ Pedestrians and non-public transit vehicles must stop on the red light and yield the right-of-way to transit vehicles.

163. **Some left turn lanes have their own traffic light to direct traffic. What does this light mean?**

   a) Pedestrians crossing the street towards the left may cross.

   b) All traffic facing the traffic light may turn left or proceed straight.

   c) Vehicles in the left turn lane may turn left while other vehicles will face a red light.

   d) This is a transit priority signal.

   ⓘ When you see this signal and you are turning left you may face other vehicles from the opposite direction also making left turns.

164. **What does a flashing amber or yellow light mean?**
    a) Slow down and drive with caution.
    b) Stop and proceed when it is safe.
    c) Stop and turn left.
    d) Stop and turn right.

ⓘ Flashing amber lights whether alone or within a traffic light warn you to slow down and proceed cautiously in the direction you are going.

165. **What does a flashing red traffic light mean?**
    a) Slow down and drive with caution.
    b) Stop and proceed when it is safe.
    c) Stop and turn left.
    d) Stop and turn right.

ⓘ Always bring your vehicle to a complete stop. Proceed into the intersection only when it is safe to do so.

166. **What does an amber or yellow light mean?**
    a) Speed up and clear the intersection so you do not block traffic when the light changes.
    b) Proceed with caution only if you cannot stop in time.
    c) Keep going and do not stop as another car can hit you from behind.
    d) There is road construction ahead so slow down and proceed with caution.

ⓘ If you can stop safely you must do so; otherwise proceed with caution. The light will be turning red soon, at which point you should be stopped.

**167. Which statement is correct regarding red lights?**

    a) You may turn right on a red light, unless otherwise posted, provided you stop first.

    b) From a one-way street to a one-way street you may turn left after slowing for a red light.

    c) If you are in a hurry you may drive through red lights with caution only if the way is clear.

    d) All of the above.

ⓘ You must always come to a complete stop at the appropriate road markings or intersection edge on a red light before making any turns.

**168. What do advanced green lights tell you?**

    a) You have the right-of-way to go in any direction in the intersection from the correct lane.

    b) They allow pedestrians to go first.

    c) A flashing green light means only vehicles turning left may do so.

    d) None of the above.

ⓘ When facing an advanced green light, oncoming traffic faces a red light, enabling you to turn left, go straight or turn right from the appropriate lane.

**169. If pedestrians face a walk signal, what should they do?**

    a) Cross the road in the direction of the symbol with the right-of-way over vehicles.

    b) Cross the road in the direction of the symbol yielding the right-of-way to vehicles.

    c) Stop and yield the right-of-way to vehicles.

    d) Cross the intersection in any direction.

ⓘ Vehicles must always be aware of their surroundings and yield the right-of-way to pedestrians crossing or those who need more time to cross.

170. **What do the white markings in this diagram represent?**
    a) Two parallel white lines at an intersection indicate a crosswalk for pedestrians.
    b) They indicate there is a one-way street to the right.
    c) These solid lines indicate there is no passing in either direction.
    d) These do not indicate anything different from the other directions.

ⓘ Intersections may have a stop line, parallel lines or a sidewalk. If these are absent, stop at the intersection edge in order to allow pedestrians to cross; and remember, no passing within 30 m of a crosswalk.

171. **What is the best way to check your blind spots?**
    a) Through your side mirrors.
    b) Through your rear view mirrors.
    c) Turning your head and doing shoulder checks.
    d) Asking your passengers to check for you.

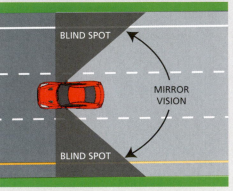

ⓘ Mirrors can help reduce the extent of blind spots but they will not get rid of them entirely; only shoulder checks will. Adjust all mirrors to minimize blind spots.

**172. How long must new drivers hold a Class G1 licence before their G1 Road Test?**

a) 6 months.

b) 12 months.

c) 18 months.

d) 2 years.

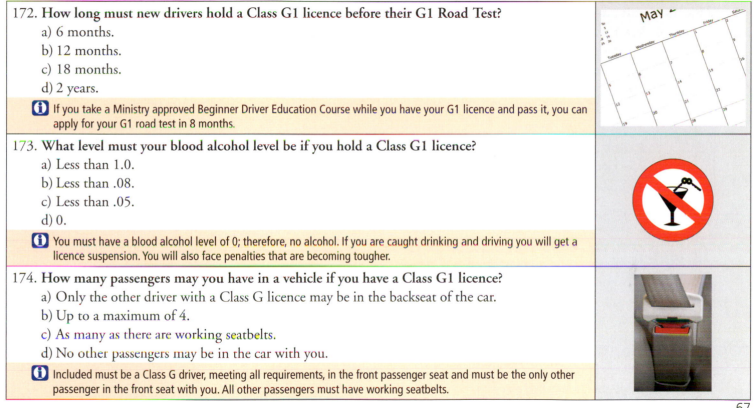

ⓘ If you take a Ministry approved Beginner Driver Education Course while you have your G1 licence and pass it, you can apply for your G1 road test in 8 months.

**173. What level must your blood alcohol level be if you hold a Class G1 licence?**

a) Less than 1.0.

b) Less than .08.

c) Less than .05.

d) 0.

ⓘ You must have a blood alcohol level of 0; therefore, no alcohol. If you are caught drinking and driving you will get a licence suspension. You will also face penalties that are becoming tougher.

**174. How many passengers may you have in a vehicle if you have a Class G1 licence?**

a) Only the other driver with a Class G licence may be in the backseat of the car.

b) Up to a maximum of 4.

c) As many as there are working seatbelts.

d) No other passengers may be in the car with you.

ⓘ Included must be a Class G driver, meeting all requirements, in the front passenger seat and must be the only other passenger in the front seat with you. All other passengers must have working seatbelts.

175. **What are the requirements of the G Class driver that may accompany a G1 driver?**
    a) The G Class driver must be in the front passenger seat.
    b) The G Class driver must have at least 4 years of driving experience.
    c) The G Class driver must have less than a .05 % blood alcohol level; 0% if under 21 years old.
    d) All of the above.

    ⓘ Included in the G Class driver's experience is any valid G2 level experience.

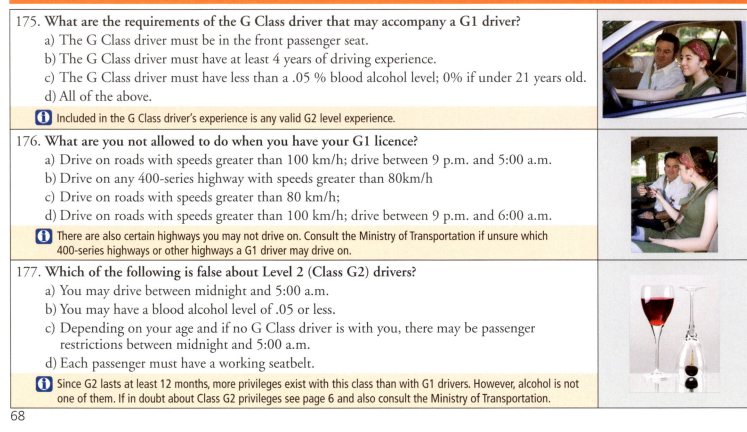

176. **What are you not allowed to do when you have your G1 licence?**
    a) Drive on roads with speeds greater than 100 km/h; drive between 9 p.m. and 5:00 a.m.
    b) Drive on any 400-series highway with speeds greater than 80km/h
    c) Drive on roads with speeds greater than 80 km/h;
    d) Drive on roads with speeds greater than 100 km/h; drive between 9 p.m. and 6:00 a.m.

    ⓘ There are also certain highways you may not drive on. Consult the Ministry of Transportation if unsure which 400-series highways or other highways a G1 driver may drive on.

177. **Which of the following is false about Level 2 (Class G2) drivers?**
    a) You may drive between midnight and 5:00 a.m.
    b) You may have a blood alcohol level of .05 or less.
    c) Depending on your age and if no G Class driver is with you, there may be passenger restrictions between midnight and 5:00 a.m.
    d) Each passenger must have a working seatbelt.

    ⓘ Since G2 lasts at least 12 months, more privileges exist with this class than with G1 drivers. However, alcohol is not one of them. If in doubt about Class G2 privileges see page 6 and also consult the Ministry of Transportation.

**178. What changes must you tell the Ministry of Transportation about?**

a) If your name has changed.

b) If your address has changed.

c) If you have a different vehicle such as a new car.

d) All of the above.

ⓘ When your name, address or any major physical change to your car occurs, you must tell the Ministry of Transportation within six days.

**179. Which of these statements is not true?**

a) You may not use a licence which has been altered.

b) You may not use an imitation licence.

c) You are allowed to have more than one Ontario licence.

d) You may not lend your licence to anyone or let anyone borrow it.

ⓘ There are licence laws that all licensed drivers must follow, or face a fine.

**180. Which of these situations may result in a driving suspension after a court order?**

a) If you have a medical condition that affects your ability to drive.

b) If you do not have your vehicle properly insured.

c) If you drive over the speed limit by 50 km/h or greater.

d) All of the above.

ⓘ You need to abide by all safety measures affecting you, others and your vehicle. Driving while under suspension will result in hefty fines, possible jail time and vehicle impoundment.

**181. If you refuse a police roadside blood alcohol screening test what can happen?**

a) You get a warning that will go on your record and you cannot refuse when asked next time.

b) You have 24 hours to show up for a test.

c) You have the option of going to the police station and taking a breathalyzer test.

d) Your licence will be suspended and you will face criminal charges.

ⓘ You must participate in a screening test. Do not avoid it by thinking you can "get off" the charges. Instead you will be charged with failing to provide a breath sample and the conviction is the same as for impaired driving.

**182. What can give you a suspension or impaired driving charge?**

a) If you hold a G1 or G2 licence and your blood alcohol level is over 0.

b) If you have a blood alcohol level over .05.

c) If you are behind the wheel of a turned-off vehicle, but your blood alcohol level is over .08.

d) All of the above.

ⓘ Having a blood alcohol content from .05–.08, known as the "warn range", will now give you a licence suspension which will increase with each occurrence. Your age and blood alcohol content also impacts suspension time.

**183. What does compulsory automobile insurance mean?**

a) You must have a valid driver's licence to drive on roads.

b) Any passenger must have a valid driver's licence.

c) You must have insurance coverage.

d) Any passengers with you must have insurance coverage.

ⓘ The Compulsory Automobile Insurance Act (CAIA) requires all Ontario drivers to carry proof that they are insured. You also have to insure all your vehicles with third party liability insurance of at least $200,000.

184. **If you change the colour of your vehicle, what are you required to do?**
    a) Tell the Driver and Vehicle Licence Issuing Office within 6 days of the change.
    b) Tell the Driver and Vehicle Licence Issuing Office within 60 days of the change.
    c) Nothing, just ensure your vehicle meets safety standards.
    d) Book an emissions test with Drive Clean.

> ℹ️ Your vehicle registration has 2 parts, licence plate and vehicle permit. The vehicle permit must have an accurate description of your vehicle, so any changes must be reported.

185. **Vehicle tires are critical for safety and they must meet which of the following standards?**
    a) Have a minimum tread of 1.5 mm.
    b) Not have any knots, exposed cords, bumps, bulges, etc., making them unsafe.
    c) Match on all 4 wheels as some combinations are illegal.
    d) All of the above.

> ℹ️ Check your owners manual for tire safety tips as each will vary depending on vehicle make and weight.

186. **If you are facing a red light and a police officer instructs traffic in the direction you are travelling to go straight, what should you do?**
    a) First stop at the intersection and then proceed.
    b) Slow down to 40 km/h and then proceed through.
    c) Follow the direction of the police officer despite what the traffic light or road sign indicates.
    d) Treat the intersection as a four-way stop.

> ℹ️ Always follow the direction of a police officer that is directing traffic.

187. **If towing a trailer that is 2.05 m wide or less, what must it have?**
   a) Two far-apart red reflectors at the back, a white licence plate light and a red tail light.
   b) Flashing yellow lights at the rear.
   c) Flashing red lights at the rear.
   d) None of the above.

> ℹ Ensure your trailer has the proper lights and reflectors. Requirements vary depending on trailer width. Never carry passengers in a moving trailer.

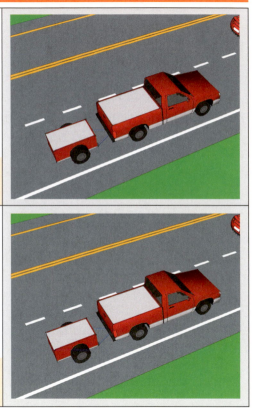

188. **Can anyone tow a trailer with a gross weight of up to 4600 kg?**
   a) As long as you have a valid G, G1, G2 or higher driver's licence.
   b) As long as you have a valid G, G1, G2 or higher driver's licence plus a trailer plate and permit.
   c) As long as your trailer has trailer plates.
   d) Only if you have your commercial vehicle licence.

> ℹ A trailer requires a special permit and plates that you need to obtain, and a one-time charge, from a Vehicle Licence Issuing Office.

**189. Which of the below infractions may cause you to receive 2 demerit points?**

a) Failure to stop for a police officer.

b) Reckless or careless driving.

c) Exceeding posted speed limits by more than 50 km/h.

d) Having passengers under 16 not wearing their seatbelts.

ⓘ Many infractions exist where you may receive a fine and/or 2 demerit points. Infraction "a" will give you 7 demerit points, while "b" and "c" will give you 6. Demerit points on your record stay for 2 years from the offence date.

**190. What if you are a G1 or G2 driver and you have 9 or more demerit points within 2 years?**

a) You must surrender your licence—your licence will be suspended for 6 days.

b) You must surrender your licence—your licence will be suspended for 60 days.

c) You must surrender your licence—your licence will be suspended for 120 days.

d) You will receive a warning letter in the mail to improve your driving.

ⓘ If you fail to surrender your licence to the Ministry of Transportation, you may lose your licence for up to 2 years. After suspension your demerit point total will be 4. Any other infractions you get will be added to this.

**191. The G2 road test includes highway driving, but before the test, what must you do?**

a) Show the instructor your G1 licence.

b) Rewrite your G1 level test and get a higher score than on your first test.

c) Sign a "Declaration of Highway Driving Experience" detailing your highway driving history.

d) Pass a colour blindness test.

ⓘ Among other details on the declaration form, you must indicate how many times in the last 3 months you drove on a highway, which highways and for how much time.

**192. What does this hand signal mean?**
- a) Driver in vehicle is slowing down or stopping.
- b) Driver in vehicle is turning right.
- c) Driver in vehicle is turning left.
- d) Driver in vehicle is exiting a highway.

ℹ If your brake lights or turn signals do not work, ensure you use proper hand signals to warn other drivers of your intentions. Use both for clarity if in doubt.

**193. What does this hand signal mean?**
- a) Driver in vehicle is slowing down or stopping.
- b) Driver in vehicle is turning right.
- c) Driver in vehicle is turning left.
- d) Driver in vehicle is exiting a highway.

ℹ If your brake lights or turn signals do not work, ensure you use proper hand signals to warn other drivers of your intentions. Use both for clarity if in doubt.

**194. What does this hand signal mean?**
- a) Driver in vehicle is slowing down or stopping.
- b) Driver in vehicle is turning right.
- c) Driver in vehicle is turning left.
- d) Driver in vehicle is exiting a highway.

ℹ If your brake lights or turn signals do not work, ensure you use proper hand signals to warn other drivers of your intentions. Use both for clarity if in doubt.

**195. As a buyer of a privately used vehicle what must you get from the seller?**

   a) The seller's licence plates and permit.

   b) The seller's driver's licence.

   c) A bill of sale.

   d) A Used Vehicle Information Package.

ⓘ The package will include details about the vehicle for the buyer's benefit. The new owner of a used vehicle has to register their new vehicle within 6 days at a Driver and Vehicle Licence Issuing Office with required documents.

**196. How many days do new Ontario residents have to register their vehicles?**

   a) 30 days.

   b) 60 days.

   c) 90 days.

   d) 120 days.

ⓘ A vehicle permit and licence plate can be obtained at a Driver and Vehicle Licence Issuing Office. Bring all required information.

**197. What does vehicle registration include?**

   a) Licence plates and a vehicle permit.

   b) Obtaining your G1 licence.

   c) Obtaining your G2 licence.

   d) None of the above.

ⓘ In Ontario, licence plates do not move with vehicles, they move with vehicle owners. When you buy a new car your existing plates go with you. All vehicle changes must be reported to a Driver and Vehicle Licence Issuing Office.

198. **What should you do when entering a freeway?**
    a) Signal, then stop to wait for an opening in traffic.
    b) Signal, then accelerate while merging smoothly into traffic.
    c) Signal, then accelerate and enter traffic quickly.
    d) Do what the vehicle ahead of you does.

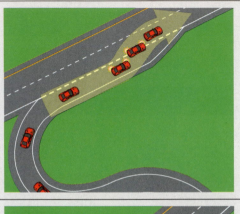

ⓘ Be sure to check your mirrors and blind spots as you move along the entrance ramp.

199. **What should you do when exiting a freeway?**
    a) Signal, then stop to wait for an opening in traffic.
    b) Signal, accelerate while merging smoothly into traffic, then proceed to the exit lane.
    c) Signal, move into the deceleration lane, reduce speed gradually and obey exit signs.
    d) Do what the vehicle ahead of you does.

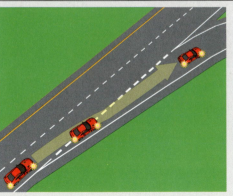

ⓘ Ensure you slow down enough when in the deceleration lane because you may not realize how fast you are going, having come off the freeway at a higher speed.

200. **What does the term "overdriving your headlights" mean?**
  a) You are leaving your lowbeam lights on too long at the risk of burning out the bulbs.
  b) You are leaving your highbeam headlights on too long at the risk of burning out the bulbs.
  c) You are driving slower than your stopping distance allows you to see.
  d) You are driving faster than your stopping distance allows you to see.

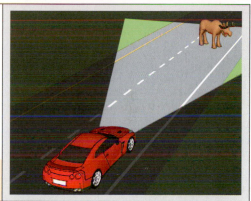

ℹ️ Slow down while driving at night to ensure you can see ahead far enough to stop appropriately.

201. **What should you do when you hear bells or sirens or see flashing lights?**
  a) Slow down, move to the far right of the roadway and stop when it is safe to do so. Do not block the shoulder if on a freeway.
  b) Slow down and move to the far left of the roadway but do not stop.
  c) Come to a complete stop wherever you are.
  d) Speed up and keep the movement of traffic going.

ℹ️ Remember to check your mirrors and blind spots and use your signals to move to the far right safely; then stop. Do not follow within 150 m of emergency vehicles.

# The Demerit Point Table of Offences

When in violation of the Highway Traffic Act, you will be fined the designated amount; you may also receive demerit points for the offence you committed. Demerit points accumulate and can lead to licence suspension. Demerit points stay on your driving record for 2 years from the date you received the offence.

The Highway Traffic Act, R.S.O, 1990 under the "Demerit Point System" provides a table of offences, shown below. For more detailed information consult the Highway Traffic Act at www.e-laws.gov.on.ca.

| Points | Short Description of Offence |
|--------|------------------------------|
| 7 | Failing to remain at the scene of an accident |
| 7 | Driver failing to stop when signalled or requested to stop by a police officer |
| 6 | Careless driving |
| 6 | Racing |
| 6 | Exceeding speed limit by 50 km/h or more |
| 6 | Failing to stop for a school bus |
| 5 | Driver of public vehicle or school bus failing to stop at railway crossings |
| 4 | Exceeding speed limit by 30 to 49 km/h |
| 4 | Following too closely |

| Points | Short Description of Offence |
|--------|------------------------------|
| 3 | Driving while using or holding a hand-held electronic device or viewing a display screen not used for driving |
| 3 | Driving through, around or under railway crossing barrier |
| 3 | Failing to yield right-of-way |
| 3 | Failing to obey a stop sign, signal light or railway crossing signal |
| 3 | Failing to obey directions of police officer |
| 3 | Driving or operating a vehicle on a closed road |
| 3 | Failing to report an accident |
| 3 | Exceeding speed limit by 16 to 29 km/h |
| 3 | Improper driving where road is divided into lanes |
| 3 | Crowding driver's seat |

| Points | Short Description of Offence |
|--------|------------------------------|
| 3 | Driving wrong way on a divided road |
| 3 | Crossing divided road where no proper crossing provided |
| 3 | Driving the wrong way in one-way street or road |
| 3 | Failing to stop at a pedestrian crossover |
| 3 | Failing to slow down and proceed with caution when approaching stopped emergency vehicle |
| 3 | Failing to move into another lane when approaching stopped emergency vehicle – if safe to do |
| 3 | Motor vehicle equipped with or carrying a speed measuring warning device |
| 3 | Improper use of high occupancy vehicle lane |
| 3 | Failing to obey traffic control stop sign |
| 3 | Failing to obey traffic control slow sign |
| 3 | Failing to obey school crossing stop sign |
| 2 | Backing on highway |
| 2 | Failing to share road |
| 2 | Improper right turn |

| Points | Short Description of Offence |
|--------|------------------------------|
| 2 | Improper left turn |
| 2 | Failing to signal |
| 2 | Unnecessary slow driving |
| 2 | Failing to lower headlamp beam |
| 2 | Improper opening of vehicle door |
| 2 | Prohibited turns |
| 2 | Towing of persons on toboggans, bicycles, skis, etc. |
| 2 | Failing to obey signs prescribed by regulation under subsection 182 (1) |
| 2 | Driver failing to properly wear seat belt |
| 2 | Driving while passenger under 16 fails to occupy position with seat belt |
| 2 | Driving while passenger under 16 fails to properly wear seat belt |
| 2 | Driver failing to ensure infant passenger is secured as prescribed |
| 2 | Driver failing to ensure toddler passenger is secured as prescribed |
| 2 | Driver failing to ensure child passenger is secured as prescribed |

# Demerit Point Consequences

## G1 or G2 Level Drivers

### 2 or More Demerit Points

A warning letter is mailed to your address.

### 6 Demerit Points

If you accumulate 6 or more demerit points you may be called in for an interview with the Ministry of Transportation where you will explain why your licence should not be suspended. Missing the interview may result in automatic licence suspension.

**Note: If you are convicted of an offence that carries 4 or more demerit points you will receive an automatic 30-day licence suspension for a first offence, a 90-day licence suspension for a second offence and any subsequent occurrences can lead to licence cancellation along with other penalties. Following this, the** demerit points will be reduced to zero on your record.

### 9 or More Demerit Points

You must surrender your licence to the Ministry of Transportation if you accu-

mulate 9 or more points within a 2-year period. At that point your licence will be suspended for 60 days from the date you surrender your licence. Failing to surrender your licence could result in your licence being suspended for 2 years. After your suspension, the number of points on your driving record will be 4 demerit points; any offences you commit in violation of the Highway Traffic Act will result in those new demerit point offences being added to your record. You then may be called for an interview again if you reach 9 or more points. At that time your licence can be suspended for 6 months.

You can surrender your licence to any ServiceOntario Centre or mail it to:

Ministry of Transportation
Driver Improvement Office
2680 Keele Street
Downsview, ON  M3M 3E6

## Fully Licensed Drivers

### 6 Demerit Points

A warning letter is mailed to your address.

### 9 Demerit Points

You may be called in for an interview with the Ministry of Transportation where you will explain why your licence should not be suspended. Missing the interview may result in automatic licence suspension. A driver re-examination may also be required.

### 15 Demerit Points

You must surrender your licence to the Ministry of Transportation; your licence will be suspended for 30 days from the surrender date for your first suspension. Failing to surrender your licence could result in your licence being suspended for 2 years. After your suspension you may also have to take a driver re-examination test to prove you have proper driving skills. This can include a knowledge and road test as well as a vision test. If you take the re-test and fail it, your

licence can be cancelled. If you pass the re-test your driving record points will be reduced to 7 demerit points. After that, any offences you commit in violation of the Highway Traffic Act will result in those new demerit point offences being added to your record. Then you may be called for an interview again. If you reach 15 or more points your licence will be suspended for 6 months.

You can surrender your licence to any ServiceOntario Centre or mail it to:

> Ministry of Transportation
> Driver Improvement Office
> 2680 Keele Street
> Downsview, ON  M3M 3E6

**Please Note: A driver re-examination is at the discretion of the Driver Improvement Office and can be asked of you, with notice, at any time.**

# The G2 Exit Test

After you have been driving the appropriate length of time, gaining the proper skills and experience to be a safe and responsible driver, you may book a G2 Exit Test.

Included during the test will be driving on a highway. As a result you will have to provide a form called "Declaration of Highway Driving Experience" to prove that you have adequate highway driving experience.

Arrive at least 30 minutes before your scheduled road test appointment. Bring a vehicle in good working order that would pass an examiner's pre-test vehicle check. Also bring your driver's licence, money for tests, and glasses if you wear them.

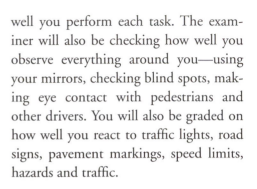

**ⓘ If you hold a G2 licence which is about to expire and you do not have adequate driving experience and/or highway driving experience you may book a G1 Exit Test to extend your licence for another 5 years.** If you fail the Level 1 road test you will not be able to drive home alone so make arrangements for this in advance.

When the examiner asks you to do a specific driving task, such as stop, turn or parallel park, he or she will be watching how you control your vehicle and how well you perform each task. The examiner will also be checking how well you observe everything around you—using your mirrors, checking blind spots, making eye contact with pedestrians and other drivers. You will also be graded on how well you react to traffic lights, road signs, pavement markings, speed limits, hazards and traffic.

Are you a defensive driver, using the **3 key principles of visibility, space, and communication?** The examiner will be checking how well you communicate with other vehicles on the road and how well you manage the space around your vehicle. Study what you have obtained from any driving course you have taken and all other sources to help you prepare for this test.

**The G2 Exit Test will test you on:**

✔ Left and right turns

✔ Stopping at intersections

✔ Driving through intersections

✔ Highway driving

✔ Changing lanes

✔ Roadside stops

✔ Curves

✔ Driving in business sections

✔ Driving in residential sections

✔ Parallel parking

✔ Three-point turns

## Left and Right Turns

### *Approaching a Turn*

#### 1. Check traffic

Look around you. Use your mirrors and, if changing lanes, check your blind spot.

#### 2. Use correct lane

Turn on the appropriate signal and move into the far left or far right lane when it is safe to do so.

#### 3. Signal

Before slowing your vehicle for the turn, put your signal on. If there are vehicles on side roads or driveways before your turn, wait until you have passed these vehicles before you signal so those drivers will not think you are turning before the intersection.

#### 4. Speed

Gradually slow down as you come to the turn. If you have a manual transmission, you can downshift into a lower gear as you reduce speed. Do not coast with your foot on the clutch.

#### 5. Space

Maintain a distance of 2 to 3 seconds behind the vehicle ahead of you while slowing down.

### *Stopping Before a Turn*
*(if required due to traffic, a stop sign, or a red light)*

#### 1. Stop

Make a complete stop and wait for traffic and lights. When the way is clear, move forward to start your turn. If you have to stop after passing the stop line and are in the intersection, do not back up.

## 2. Space

If a vehicle is ahead of you at an inter-section, ensure you have enough space to pass the vehicle without backing up. This cushion of space lets you pull out if the vehicle stalls; it reduces risk of collision if the vehicle rolls backward; and it mini-mizes or avoids a collision if you are hit from behind.

Leave enough space in front of your vehicle so that if the car in front of you stalls you can pull around that vehicle without backing up.

## 3. Stop line

If there are no vehicles ahead of you as you approach an intersection with a red light or stop sign, stop behind the marked stop line. If there is no marked stop line, stop at the crosswalk, whether it is marked or not. If there is no cross-walk, stop at the edge of the sidewalk. And if there is no sidewalk, stop at the edge of the intersection.

## 4. Wheels

Make sure your wheels are straight as you wait to make your left turn. This ensures that your vehicle will not get pushed into oncoming traffic. When waiting to make a right turn, also keep your wheels straight so you do not hit pedestrians

if you get hit from behind. At large inter-sections angle your vehicle so that no other car can fit between you and the curb.

## The Actual Turn

### 1. Traffic check

Before pulling into the intersection, look left, ahead, and right to make sure that the way is clear. If you are unsure about who has the right-of-way, try to make eye contact with the drivers or pedestrians in question. Check your blind spot before turning in case it is possible for another vehicle to overtake you. If a pedestrian or vehicle with the right-of-way has to get out of your way, then you have not checked traffic properly.

### 2. Hands

Your risk of collision is greatest when turning so to maintain control of your vehicle keep both hands on the steering wheel throughout the turn.

### 3. Gears

If you are driving a vehicle with manual transmission, you maintain more control when turning by not changing gears. If necessary, shift gears after the vehicle is moving but before the turn. If the intersection is wider than four lanes, you may shift gears in order to not slow down the general flow of traffic.

### 4. Speed

Start moving within 4 to 5 seconds once you have ensured it is safe. Drive slow enough to maintain control of your vehicle and increase speed as you complete the turn.

### 5. Entering new lane

Once you have cleared the intersection, enter your corresponding lane without going over lane markings or curbs.

## Completing the Turn

### 1. Lane

Enter the lane that you turned from. When turning left onto a multi-lane road, turn into the left lane. Return to normal speed and move into the curb lane when it is safe to do so. When turning right, move into the right lane. If it is blocked with parked vehicles, move over to the next available lane.

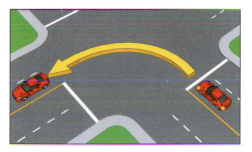

### 2. Traffic check

Check your mirrors on the new road as you return to normal speed. Make yourself fully aware of the traffic on this street; many conditions may be different from the street you turned from.

### 3. Speed

Return to normal traffic speed but adapt and blend in with the traffic of the new road. Remember to not exceed the speed limit.

## Stopping at Intersections

### The Approach

#### 1. Traffic check

Before you slow down, take a look at everything around you. Check traffic behind you by looking into all mirrors.

#### 2. Speed

As you near the intersection, gradually reduce speed. If you have a manual transmission, downshift into a lower gear as you reduce speed. Do not coast by keeping your foot on the clutch.

#### 3. Space

Stay at least 2 to 3 seconds behind the vehicle ahead of you.

### The Stop

#### 1. Stop

Make a complete stop without rolling forward or backward. When traffic allows, move forward to ensure the way is clear and start moving across the intersection. If you need to stop after passing the stop line and are in the intersection, do not back up.

#### 2. Space

If a vehicle is ahead of you at an intersection, ensure you have enough space to pass the vehicle without backing up. This cushion of space lets you pull out if the vehicle stalls; it reduces the risk of a collision if the vehicle rolls backward; and it minimizes or avoids a collision if you are hit from behind.

#### 3. Stop line

If there are no vehicles ahead of you as you approach an intersection with a red light or stop sign, stop behind the marked stop line. If there is no marked stop line, stop at the crosswalk, whether it is marked or

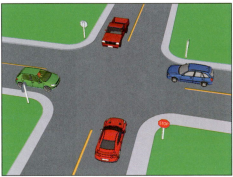

not. If there is no crosswalk, stop at the edge of the sidewalk. If there is no sidewalk, stop at the edge of the intersection.

## Driving Through

### 1. Traffic check

Before entering an intersection, look left, ahead, and right to make sure nothing is in your path. If you are unsure about who has the right-of-way, try to make eye contact with the drivers or pedestrians in question. If a pedestrian or vehicle with the right-of-way has to get out of your way, then you have not checked traffic properly.

### 2. Hands

Your risk of collision is greatest when crossing the intersection so to maintain control of your vehicle keep both hands on the steering wheel.

### 3. Gears

If you are driving a vehicle with manual transmission, you will maintain more control by not changing gears while crossing an intersection. If necessary, shift gears after the vehicle is moving but before it is far into the intersection. If the intersection is wider than four lanes, you may shift gears as long as you do not slow down traffic

### 4. Traffic check

After going through the intersection, check your mirrors as you return to normal speed and make yourself fully aware of all traffic.

### 5. Speed

Start moving within 4 to 5 seconds once you have ensured it is safe. Return to normal traffic speed but adapt and blend in with traffic. Remember to not exceed the speed limit.

## Driving Through Intersections

### The Approach

### 1. Traffic check

As you near the intersection, look left and right to see if there is any traffic on the intersecting road. If it is necessary to slow down, check on the traffic situation in your rear-view mirror.

### 2. Speed

Maintain your speed when proceeding through the intersection unless you see that traffic may cross your path. If that is the case, reduce speed or hold your foot over the brake pedal so you are prepared to stop if necessary. Be extra alert for pedestrians and vehicles coming into the intersection, as well as vehicles approaching at higher speeds.

### 3. Space

Maintain a distance of 2 to 3 seconds behind the vehicle ahead of you.

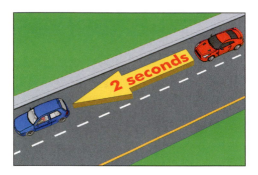

## Driving Through

### 1. Lane

Stay within your lane. Do not change lanes or drive across lane markings in the intersection. Slow down or stop if your lane is blocked by a left-turning vehicle or a vehicle turning into the intersection

from the right.

### 2. Hands

Your risk of collision is greatest when crossing the intersection so to maintain control of your vehicle keep both hands on the steering wheel.

### 3. Gears

If you are driving a vehicle with manual transmission, maintain more control when crossing the intersection by not changing gears. If necessary, shift gears after the vehicle is moving but before it is in the intersection. If the intersection is wider than four lanes, you may shift gears as long as you do not slow down traffic. Generally, the less gear shifting you do the more vehicle control you will have.

### 4. Traffic check

If you had to slow down at the

intersection, check your mirrors before resuming normal traffic speed.

## The Highway

### Entering

### 1. Traffic check

When driving on a highway entrance ramp, as soon as you see highway traffic approaching behind you, check your mirrors and blind spot to find a safe place to merge. You also have to be well aware of vehicles in front of you. Make sure you are a safe distance behind. Keep checking your mirrors, your blind spot, and the vehicle ahead of you until you can merge safely.

### 2. Signal

Turn your signal on as soon as highway traffic can see your vehicle on the ramp.

### 3. Space

While merging with highway traffic, stay at least 2 to 3 seconds behind the vehicle ahead of you. Do not merge right beside another vehicle or into someone's blind spot. Sometimes traffic moves at such high speed that it is hard to maintain an ideal following distance. Adjust your speed for the best possible spacing between your vehicle and others and keep inside the lane markings.

### 4. Speed

Merging on the highway is a combination of slowing down and speeding up. Prior to the merge, you will enter via a curving entrance ramp. Use a speed that is not too fast for the curve. Then, once in the straight acceleration lane, speed up to match the flow of highway traffic. During the merge, control your speed so that you blend smoothly with the rest of the traffic.

### 5. Merge

Merge smoothly with highway traffic to the centre of the nearest highway lane.

### 6. Turn off signal

Once you have merged, turn off your signal.

A  Check mirrors and blind spots for space.
B  Signal and check for space again.
C  Steer into lane.
D  Turn off signal.

ACCELERATE and MERGE
SLOW  SLOW

## Driving Along

### 1. Traffic check

While driving in the same lane, keep a constant check on the traffic around you. Check your mirrors every 5 to 10 seconds.

### 2. Speed

Maintain a steady speed. Exceeding the speed limit is to be avoided, as is driving too slowly. Be alert. Make sure you can see where you will be 12 to 15 seconds ahead, anticipating dangerous situations or obstacles. Adjust your speed accordingly.

### 3. Space

Keep at least a 2- to 3-second distance behind the vehicle ahead of you. Make this distance even greater or change lanes if another vehicle is following you too closely from behind. Try to maintain space on all sides of your vehicle and avoid driving in the blind spots of other vehicles. Large vehicles block your view so it is advisable not to drive behind them.

## Exiting

### 1. Traffic check

Check your mirrors and look left and right before moving into the exit lane. If there is a right lane beside you, check your blind spot.

### 2. Signal

Turn your signal on before reaching the exit lane.

### 3. Exit lane

Using smooth movement and staying inside the lane markings, begin to enter the exit lane. Do not cross solid lines if there is more than one exit lane.

### 4. Speed

Wait until you are completely in the exit lane before slowing down. Gradually decrease speed in the exit lane and on the exit ramp, ensuring that you do not go too fast on the curve. Vehicles with manual transmissions should downshift while reducing speed.

### 5. Space

Maintain a 2- to 3-second distance behind the vehicle ahead of you.

### 6. Turn signal off

Once on the exit ramp, turn off your signal.

## Changing Lanes

### 1. Traffic check

First, make a visual sweep of everything around you. Look ahead, in the mirrors, and check your blind spot. If you are on a multi-lane highway, make sure another vehicle in the far lane is not moving into the same lane you are.

### 2. Signal

When there is enough room for you to change lanes, put your signal on. Check your blind spot once more before moving into the other lane. Your signal alerts drivers behind you as to what you want to do. Even if there does not appear to be enough room due to traffic to make a lane change, with your signal on, traffic behind you will know your intentions.

### 3. Space

Make sure you have a 2- to 3-second distance behind the vehicle ahead of you. If there is another lane beside the one you are in, take care not to move into it and beside another vehicle. Do not move into the blind spot of another vehicle, either.

### 4. Speed

Adjust your speed so that you are moving with the flow of traffic in the new lane without exceeding the speed limit.

### 5. Change

Gradually and smoothly move into the centre of the new lane.

### 6. Hands

Keep both hands on the steering wheel for best control as you change lanes.

### 7. Turn off signal

Once you have changed lanes, turn off your signal.

## The Roadside Stop

### The Approach

### 1. Traffic check

Check your mirrors before slowing down. Ensure there are no signs indicating it is illegal to make a stop. Next, check traffic approaching your vehicle from the front and rear, allowing for enough space in both directions for a safe move. A 150 m distance in both directions is recommended. Check your blind spot if there is a possibility of traffic or pedestrians passing you on the right.

### 2. Signal

Before slowing down, put your signal on. If there are vehicles on side roads or driveways between you and where you plan to stop, wait until you have passed them so those drivers do not think you will turn before the stopping point.

### 3. Speed

Gradually slow down as you approach the stop. If you have a manual transmission, you may downshift into a lower gear as you reduce speed. Do not coast by keeping your foot on the clutch.

### 4. Position

Stop no more than 30 cm away from the curb and keep parallel to it. If there is no curb, pull over as far as you can from the travelled part of the road. Make sure you do not block any entrances or other traffic.

## The Stop

### 1. Signal

Turn your signal lights off and turn on your four-way hazard lights.

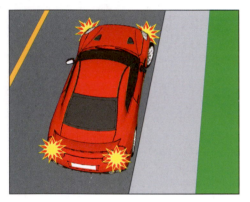

### 2. Park

Set your vehicle in park with the parking brake. If you have a manual transmission put the parking brake on and shift into neutral if you are not turning off the ignition. Otherwise, shift into low or reverse if shutting down the engine and then set the parking brake. Position wheels in the correct direction to ensure the vehicle does not roll.

## Resume

### 1. Start

Turn the engine on again. Release the parking brake and shift into the correct gear.

### 2. Signal

Turn off your four-way hazard lights and then turn on your left turn signal.

### 3. Traffic check

Before pulling onto the road in the nearest lane, check your mirrors and your left blind spot.

### 4. Speed

Accelerate smoothly as you return to normal traffic speed but adapt and blend in with the traffic of the new road. Remember not to exceed the speed limit.

### 5. Turn off signal

Once back on the road, turn your signal off.

## Curves

### 1. Speed

Before embarking on a curve, it helps to determine a safe speed. To do this, look for signs that display the speed; determine how sharp the curve is; and consider the type of road surface you are driving on. The safe speed should be achieved by the time you are 30 m into the curve. If you can not see all the way around the curve, slow down. The curve may be tighter than you think or oncoming traffic could be approaching closely.

**Make sure you slow down before the curve to avoid braking in it.** Once in the curve, maintain a slow, steady speed. As you approach the end of the curve, accelerate to return to normal speed. Vehicles with manual transmissions should not shift gears in the curve. This will provide more control and reduce the possibility of your wheels locking while downshifting.

## 2. Lane

Once you have entered the curve, look as far as you can around it. This will help you drive in a smooth line while staying in the centre of the lane. Looking only at the road right ahead of you makes you likely to veer across the lane and forces you to constantly correct your steering.

## Business Sections

### 1. Traffic check

Roads in business areas are much more cluttered than other roads. Be aware. Vehicles and pedestrians can enter the road from a number of areas. There are more pedestrian crossings, as well as entrances to businesses, institutions and parking lots. Railway crossings and bicycles may also be part of a business section. Make sure you look left and right at all entrances to check for vehicles or pedestrians that may be entering the road.

### 2. Mirror check

Check your mirrors every 5 to 10 seconds while driving. If traffic is heavy or if vehicles are travelling at different speeds, check mirrors more frequently.

### 3. Lane

Drive in the safest lane (usually the curb

lane). If the curb lane is blocked with parked cars or traffic, drive in the centre lane. Stay in the middle of your lane.

Plan where you will be in the next 12 to 15 seconds by looking ahead and change lanes if you need to avoid any obstacles.

### 4. Speed

Drive at a steady speed. Avoid driving too slowly or exceeding the speed limit. Plan where you will be in the next 12 to 15 seconds by looking ahead and change speed if you need to avoid any obstacles.

### 5. Space

Keep a minimum 2- to 3-second distance between you and the vehicle ahead of you. Make this distance even greater if you are being followed too closely. Try to maintain space on all sides of your vehicle, especially on multi-lane roads, and avoid driving in the blind spots of other vehicles. In slow traffic, large vehicles may block your view of what is ahead so avoid driving behind them. When you stop behind another vehicle, allow enough space to see its rear wheels so that you can pull around it without having to back up.

## Residential Sections

### 1. Traffic check

On residential streets, be aware of pedestrian crossings and entrances to schools, driveways and stores. On rural roads, be aware of entrances to farms, homes, businesses and industrial sites. Always look to your left and right, be on the lookout for pedestrians or vehicles entering the roadway.

### 2. Mirror check

Check your mirrors every 5 to 10 seconds while driving. If traffic is heavy or if vehicles are travelling at different speeds, check mirrors more frequently.

### 3. Lane

Stay in the centre of the lane. Some streets will not have lane markings, in which case you should stay in the centre of the travelled part of the road away from pedestrians and parked vehicles. If you are approaching a hill or curve where you are unable to see ahead, stay as far right as possible to avoid a collision in case an oncoming vehicle is over the centre line. Plan where you will be in the next 12 to 15 seconds by looking ahead and change lanes if you need to avoid any obstacles.

### 4. Speed

Drive at a steady speed. Avoid driving too slowly or exceeding the speed limit. Plan where you will be in the next 12 to 15 seconds by looking ahead and change speed if you need to avoid any obstacles.

### 5. Space

Keep a minimum 2- to 3-second distance behind you and the vehicle ahead of you. Make this distance even greater if you are being followed too closely. Try to maintain space on all sides of your vehicle, especially on multi-lane roads, and avoid driving in the blind spots of other vehicles. In slow traffic, large vehicles may block your view of what is ahead so avoid driving behind them. When you stop behind another vehicle, allow enough space to see its rear wheels so that you can pull around it without having to back up.

## Parallel Parking

### The Approach

### 1. Traffic check

Check your mirrors before slowing down. Check your blind spot before getting into position to back up.

### 2. Signal

Before slowing down, turn on your signal. If there are vehicles on side roads or

driveways between you and where you plan to stop, wait until you have passed them so those drivers will not think you are turning before your parking position.

### 3. Speed

Gradually slow down. If you have a manual transmission, reduce speed while you downshift into a lower gear. Do not coast with your foot on the clutch.

### 4. Stop

Stop parallel to the parked vehicle in front of the empty parking space or if no vehicle is there stop beside where it would be. Make sure there is at least 60 cm between your vehicle and the parked vehicle. Stop when you are completely in front of the empty parking space.

## Parking

### 1. Traffic check

Before you put your vehicle in reverse, check your mirrors and both blind spots to ensure that nothing is in your way. Do not reverse until the way is clear.

### 2. Back up

Begin to back up into the empty space while turning the steering wheel toward the curb. When you are about halfway in, steer your vehicle in line with the curb. Once in the space, move your vehicle forward and/or backward until it fits within the pavement markings. Whether there are pavement markings or not, make sure you allow enough room for vehicles in front of and behind you to get out of their parking space. While parking, never hit the curb or bump other vehicles. If there is no curb, park on the untravelled part of the road.

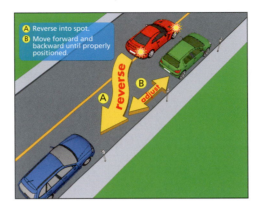

A  Reverse into spot.
B  Move forward and backward until properly positioned.

### 3. Park

Shift your vehicle into park and set the parking brake. If you have a manual transmission, shift into low or reverse and turn off the engine and set the parking brake. Position wheels in the correct direction to ensure your vehicle does not roll.

## Resume

### 1. Start

Turn your engine on and release the parking brake. Shift into the appropriate gear to get back on the road.

### 2. Signal

Turn on your left signal light.

### 3. Traffic check

Check your mirrors and blind spot before pulling out of the parking space.

### 4. Speed

Accelerate smoothly as you return to normal traffic speed but adapt and blend in with traffic. Remember not to exceed the speed limit.

### 5. Turn off signal

Once back on the road, turn your signal off.

## Three-Point Turn

### *The Approach*

#### 1. Traffic check

Check traffic in front and behind you before slowing down. Check your blind spot if necessary.

#### 2. Signal

Before slowing down, turn on your signal. If there are vehicles on side roads or driveways between you and where you plan to stop, wait until you have passed them so those drivers will not think you are turning too early.

#### 3. Speed

Gradually slow down. If you have a manual transmission, you may downshift into a lower gear as you reduce speed. Do not coast with your foot on the clutch.

#### 4. Position

Stop parallel to the curb, ensuring you are no more than 30 cm away from it. If there is no curb, stop as far as you can off the travelled part of the road. Make sure you do not block any entrances or other traffic.

### *Turn Around*

#### 1. Traffic check

Before beginning your turn, check your mirrors and blind spot. Wait until you are certain the way is clear. Check traffic in both directions each time you stop while turning.

#### 2. Signal

Turn your left signal on before you begin turning.

#### 3. Turn around

Turn your steering wheel sharply to the left. Steer your vehicle slowly across the road. Once you are at the far left side of the road, stop and shift into reverse. Turn your steering wheel sharply to the right and reverse so that your vehicle is now facing the opposite direction. Stop and shift into forward gear. Use as much of the road as possible so that you only reverse once. Ensure you do not reverse into the curb or over the edge of the road.

### *Resume*

#### 1. Traffic check

Check your mirrors before accelerating.

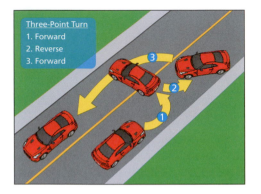

Three-Point Turn
1. Forward
2. Reverse
3. Forward

## 2. Speed

Accelerate smoothly as you return to normal traffic speed but adapt and blend in with traffic. If your vehicle has manual transmission, shift gears as speed increases. Remember not to exceed the speed limit.

**Driving Tips for All Seasons**

# Get a
# Spring
## tune-UP

Canada's winters can wreak havoc on your vehicle. So get a tune-up. The more checks, the better your vehicle will run. The extra cost of more preventative checks will save you costly repair bills later. Some things to check include: spark plugs, filters, cooling system, brakes, oil, wiper blades, fluids and proper tread on tires.

# Practice Test Form

1. ❏ a ❏ b ❏ c ❏ d
2. ❏ a ❏ b ❏ c ❏ d
3. ❏ a ❏ b ❏ c ❏ d
4. ❏ a ❏ b ❏ c ❏ d
5. ❏ a ❏ b ❏ c ❏ d
6. ❏ a ❏ b ❏ c ❏ d
7. ❏ a ❏ b ❏ c ❏ d
8. ❏ a ❏ b ❏ c ❏ d
9. ❏ a ❏ b ❏ c ❏ d
10. ❏ a ❏ b ❏ c ❏ d
11. ❏ a ❏ b ❏ c ❏ d
12. ❏ a ❏ b ❏ c ❏ d
13. ❏ a ❏ b ❏ c ❏ d
14. ❏ a ❏ b ❏ c ❏ d
15. ❏ a ❏ b ❏ c ❏ d
16. ❏ a ❏ b ❏ c ❏ d
17. ❏ a ❏ b ❏ c ❏ d
18. ❏ a ❏ b ❏ c ❏ d
19. ❏ a ❏ b ❏ c ❏ d
20. ❏ a ❏ b ❏ c ❏ d

21. ❏ a ❏ b ❏ c ❏ d
22. ❏ a ❏ b ❏ c ❏ d
23. ❏ a ❏ b ❏ c ❏ d
24. ❏ a ❏ b ❏ c ❏ d
25. ❏ a ❏ b ❏ c ❏ d
26. ❏ a ❏ b ❏ c ❏ d
27. ❏ a ❏ b ❏ c ❏ d
28. ❏ a ❏ b ❏ c ❏ d
29. ❏ a ❏ b ❏ c ❏ d
30. ❏ a ❏ b ❏ c ❏ d
31. ❏ a ❏ b ❏ c ❏ d
32. ❏ a ❏ b ❏ c ❏ d
33. ❏ a ❏ b ❏ c ❏ d
34. ❏ a ❏ b ❏ c ❏ d
35. ❏ a ❏ b ❏ c ❏ d
36. ❏ a ❏ b ❏ c ❏ d
37. ❏ a ❏ b ❏ c ❏ d
38. ❏ a ❏ b ❏ c ❏ d
39. ❏ a ❏ b ❏ c ❏ d
40. ❏ a ❏ b ❏ c ❏ d

41. ❏ a ❏ b ❏ c ❏ d
42. ❏ a ❏ b ❏ c ❏ d
43. ❏ a ❏ b ❏ c ❏ d
44. ❏ a ❏ b ❏ c ❏ d
45. ❏ a ❏ b ❏ c ❏ d
46. ❏ a ❏ b ❏ c ❏ d
47. ❏ a ❏ b ❏ c ❏ d
48. ❏ a ❏ b ❏ c ❏ d
49. ❏ a ❏ b ❏ c ❏ d
50. ❏ a ❏ b ❏ c ❏ d
51. ❏ a ❏ b ❏ c ❏ d
52. ❏ a ❏ b ❏ c ❏ d
53. ❏ a ❏ b ❏ c ❏ d
54. ❏ a ❏ b ❏ c ❏ d
55. ❏ a ❏ b ❏ c ❏ d
56. ❏ a ❏ b ❏ c ❏ d
57. ❏ a ❏ b ❏ c ❏ d
58. ❏ a ❏ b ❏ c ❏ d
59. ❏ a ❏ b ❏ c ❏ d
60. ❏ a ❏ b ❏ c ❏ d

61. ❏ a ❏ b ❏ c ❏ d
62. ❏ a ❏ b ❏ c ❏ d
63. ❏ a ❏ b ❏ c ❏ d
64. ❏ a ❏ b ❏ c ❏ d
65. ❏ a ❏ b ❏ c ❏ d
66. ❏ a ❏ b ❏ c ❏ d
67. ❏ a ❏ b ❏ c ❏ d
68. ❏ a ❏ b ❏ c ❏ d
69. ❏ a ❏ b ❏ c ❏ d
70. ❏ a ❏ b ❏ c ❏ d
71. ❏ a ❏ b ❏ c ❏ d
72. ❏ a ❏ b ❏ c ❏ d
73. ❏ a ❏ b ❏ c ❏ d
74. ❏ a ❏ b ❏ c ❏ d
75. ❏ a ❏ b ❏ c ❏ d
76. ❏ a ❏ b ❏ c ❏ d
77. ❏ a ❏ b ❏ c ❏ d
78. ❏ a ❏ b ❏ c ❏ d
79. ❏ a ❏ b ❏ c ❏ d
80. ❏ a ❏ b ❏ c ❏ d

81. ❏ a ❏ b ❏ c ❏ d
82. ❏ a ❏ b ❏ c ❏ d
83. ❏ a ❏ b ❏ c ❏ d
84. ❏ a ❏ b ❏ c ❏ d
85. ❏ a ❏ b ❏ c ❏ d
86. ❏ a ❏ b ❏ c ❏ d
87. ❏ a ❏ b ❏ c ❏ d
88. ❏ a ❏ b ❏ c ❏ d
89. ❏ a ❏ b ❏ c ❏ d
90. ❏ a ❏ b ❏ c ❏ d
91. ❏ a ❏ b ❏ c ❏ d
92. ❏ a ❏ b ❏ c ❏ d
93. ❏ a ❏ b ❏ c ❏ d
94. ❏ a ❏ b ❏ c ❏ d
95. ❏ a ❏ b ❏ c ❏ d
96. ❏ a ❏ b ❏ c ❏ d
97. ❏ a ❏ b ❏ c ❏ d
98. ❏ a ❏ b ❏ c ❏ d
99. ❏ a ❏ b ❏ c ❏ d
100. ❏ a ❏ b ❏ c ❏ d

101. ❑ a ❑ b ❑ c ❑ d
102. ❑ a ❑ b ❑ c ❑ d
103. ❑ a ❑ b ❑ c ❑ d
104. ❑ a ❑ b ❑ c ❑ d
105. ❑ a ❑ b ❑ c ❑ d
106. ❑ a ❑ b ❑ c ❑ d
107. ❑ a ❑ b ❑ c ❑ d
108. ❑ a ❑ b ❑ c ❑ d
109. ❑ a ❑ b ❑ c ❑ d
110. ❑ a ❑ b ❑ c ❑ d
111. ❑ a ❑ b ❑ c ❑ d
112. ❑ a ❑ b ❑ c ❑ d
113. ❑ a ❑ b ❑ c ❑ d
114. ❑ a ❑ b ❑ c ❑ d
115. ❑ a ❑ b ❑ c ❑ d
116. ❑ a ❑ b ❑ c ❑ d
117. ❑ a ❑ b ❑ c ❑ d
118. ❑ a ❑ b ❑ c ❑ d
119. ❑ a ❑ b ❑ c ❑ d
120. ❑ a ❑ b ❑ c ❑ d

121. ❑ a ❑ b ❑ c ❑ d
122. ❑ a ❑ b ❑ c ❑ d
123. ❑ a ❑ b ❑ c ❑ d
124. ❑ a ❑ b ❑ c ❑ d
125. ❑ a ❑ b ❑ c ❑ d
126. ❑ a ❑ b ❑ c ❑ d
127. ❑ a ❑ b ❑ c ❑ d
128. ❑ a ❑ b ❑ c ❑ d
129. ❑ a ❑ b ❑ c ❑ d
130. ❑ a ❑ b ❑ c ❑ d
131. ❑ a ❑ b ❑ c ❑ d
132. ❑ a ❑ b ❑ c ❑ d
133. ❑ a ❑ b ❑ c ❑ d
134. ❑ a ❑ b ❑ c ❑ d
135. ❑ a ❑ b ❑ c ❑ d
136. ❑ a ❑ b ❑ c ❑ d
137. ❑ a ❑ b ❑ c ❑ d
138. ❑ a ❑ b ❑ c ❑ d
139. ❑ a ❑ b ❑ c ❑ d
140. ❑ a ❑ b ❑ c ❑ d

141. ❑ a ❑ b ❑ c ❑ d
142. ❑ a ❑ b ❑ c ❑ d
143. ❑ a ❑ b ❑ c ❑ d
144. ❑ a ❑ b ❑ c ❑ d
145. ❑ a ❑ b ❑ c ❑ d
146. ❑ a ❑ b ❑ c ❑ d
147. ❑ a ❑ b ❑ c ❑ d
148. ❑ a ❑ b ❑ c ❑ d
149. ❑ a ❑ b ❑ c ❑ d
150. ❑ a ❑ b ❑ c ❑ d
151. ❑ a ❑ b ❑ c ❑ d
152. ❑ a ❑ b ❑ c ❑ d
153. ❑ a ❑ b ❑ c ❑ d
154. ❑ a ❑ b ❑ c ❑ d
155. ❑ a ❑ b ❑ c ❑ d
156. ❑ a ❑ b ❑ c ❑ d
157. ❑ a ❑ b ❑ c ❑ d
158. ❑ a ❑ b ❑ c ❑ d
159. ❑ a ❑ b ❑ c ❑ d
160. ❑ a ❑ b ❑ c ❑ d
161. ❑ a ❑ b ❑ c ❑ d

162. ❑ a ❑ b ❑ c ❑ d
163. ❑ a ❑ b ❑ c ❑ d
164. ❑ a ❑ b ❑ c ❑ d
165. ❑ a ❑ b ❑ c ❑ d
166. ❑ a ❑ b ❑ c ❑ d
167. ❑ a ❑ b ❑ c ❑ d
168. ❑ a ❑ b ❑ c ❑ d
169. ❑ a ❑ b ❑ c ❑ d
170. ❑ a ❑ b ❑ c ❑ d
171. ❑ a ❑ b ❑ c ❑ d
172. ❑ a ❑ b ❑ c ❑ d
173. ❑ a ❑ b ❑ c ❑ d
174. ❑ a ❑ b ❑ c ❑ d
175. ❑ a ❑ b ❑ c ❑ d
176. ❑ a ❑ b ❑ c ❑ d
177. ❑ a ❑ b ❑ c ❑ d
178. ❑ a ❑ b ❑ c ❑ d
179. ❑ a ❑ b ❑ c ❑ d
180. ❑ a ❑ b ❑ c ❑ d
181. ❑ a ❑ b ❑ c ❑ d

182. ❑ a ❑ b ❑ c ❑ d
183. ❑ a ❑ b ❑ c ❑ d
184. ❑ a ❑ b ❑ c ❑ d
185. ❑ a ❑ b ❑ c ❑ d
186. ❑ a ❑ b ❑ c ❑ d
187. ❑ a ❑ b ❑ c ❑ d
188. ❑ a ❑ b ❑ c ❑ d
189. ❑ a ❑ b ❑ c ❑ d
190. ❑ a ❑ b ❑ c ❑ d
191. ❑ a ❑ b ❑ c ❑ d
192. ❑ a ❑ b ❑ c ❑ d
193. ❑ a ❑ b ❑ c ❑ d
194. ❑ a ❑ b ❑ c ❑ d
195. ❑ a ❑ b ❑ c ❑ d
196. ❑ a ❑ b ❑ c ❑ d
197. ❑ a ❑ b ❑ c ❑ d
198. ❑ a ❑ b ❑ c ❑ d
199. ❑ a ❑ b ❑ c ❑ d
200. ❑ a ❑ b ❑ c ❑ d
201. ❑ a ❑ b ❑ c ❑ d

# Notes:

# Pedestrian Crossovers and School Crossings—New Law Effective January 1, 2016

Drivers must come to a complete stop and yield the entire roadway at pedestrian crossovers and school crossings where there is a crossing guard present displaying a school crossing stop sign. The new law also applies to new types of pedestrian crossovers.

A Pedestrian Crossover

B School Crossing

C Pedestrian Crossover

D Pedestrian Crosswalk

## New Law Applies at:

A Pedestrian Crossovers

B School Crossings with a school crossing guard present displaying a school crossing stop sign

C New types of Pedestrian Crossovers

## New Law Does Not Apply at:

D Crosswalks, whether there are traffic lights or not (unless a school crossing guard is present)

# Customer Response Card

Thank you for purchasing the Ontario Driver's Study Guide!

Our goal is to provide you with the information you need to pass Ontario driving tests.

Please complete the information below so we will be able to serve you and others better in the future. We value your comments and suggestions for improvements. Let us know what you think. Comments can also be e-mailed to: feedback@cccmaps.com.

(This information is for internal use ONLY and will NOT be distributed or sold to any external third party.)

Your Name: _____

Address: _____

City: _____ Postal Code: _____

Phone Number: _____ E-mail: _____

1. Age Group:

 [ ] 16-24   [ ] 25-31   [ ] 32-40   [ ] 41-50   [ ] 51-70   [ ] 71-79   [ ] 80+

2. Where did you purchase your Driver's Study Guide? (store name & location) _____

_____

3. What did you like best about the Driver's Study Guide? _____

_____

4. What did you like least about it? _____

_____

5. What would you add/change in the Driver's Study Guide? _____

_____

6. Did you pass your applicable test after reading the Driver's Study Guide?

 [ ] YES   [ ] NO

7. Why do you think you passed or failed? _____

_____

8. Please provide any additional comments or suggestions you have: _____

_____

## Fax or mail to:

Canadian Cartographics Corporation
70 Bloor Street East
Oshawa, Ontario
L1H 3M2

Fax: 905.723.6677

r.12

# cccmaps.com

## Student Edition World Atlas

## $5.95

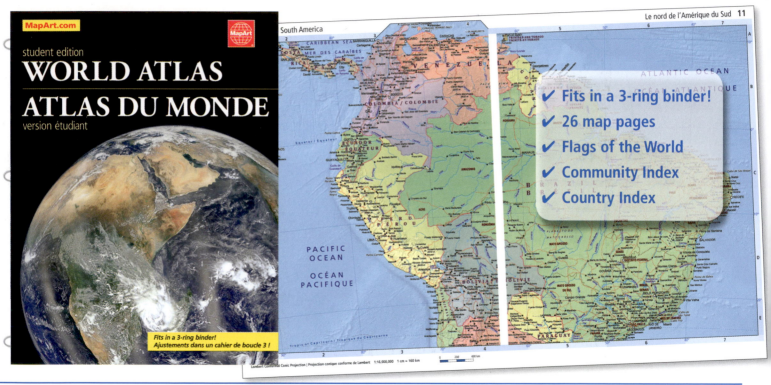

MapArt.com

### student edition
# WORLD ATLAS
# ATLAS DU MONDE
version étudiant

Fits in a 3-ring binder!
Ajustements dans un cahier de boucle 3 !

Le nord de l'Amérique du Sud 11

✔ Fits in a 3-ring binder!
✔ 26 map pages
✔ Flags of the World
✔ Community Index
✔ Country Index